PRAISE FOR LAWRENCE OSBORNE'S
THE WET AND THE DRY

"Mr. Osborne is a superb travel writer, one who, like Evelyn Waugh, can size up a locale at almost a glance. This intoxicating book has political as well as sensual overtones. It's about how East and West think about alcohol; quite often it's about one man's search for his 6:10 p.m. martini in some very unlikely locations."

—**Dwight Garner, *New York Times***

"Instantly among the best nonfiction volumes about drinking that we have . . . Mr. Osborne comes across in *The Wet and the Dry* as a real human being indeed—a complicated man mixing complicated feelings into fizzy, adult, intoxicating prose."

—***New York Times***

"A bracing, brilliant meditation on everything from the universal qualities that make a good bar to the mysteries of vodka . . . Relentlessly sharp-minded."

—***Boston Globe***

"In this entertaining travel essay/memoir, [Osborne] combines both of his loves with a combination of sparkling prose and insightful observations. . . . Endlessly fascinating."

—***Chicago Tribune***

"Osborne elicits some profound and harrowing reflections. . . . From Dubai to Beirut, Islamabad to Brooklyn, Osborne's meditations on fermentation and distillation induce a host of refreshing, taut, timeless unmoorings."

—***Publishers Weekly*** **(starred review)**

"A cosmopolitan and prodigious drinker conducts a tour to selected locales where alcohol flows easily and to others where such spirits are strictly forbidden. . . . Rakish, rich, and nicely served."

—***Kirkus Reviews***

Also by the Author

The Forgiven

Bangkok Days

The Naked Tourist

The Accidental Connoisseur

American Normal

The Poisoned Embrace

Paris Dreambook

Ania Malina

LAWRENCE OSBORNE

A Drinker's Journey

THE WET AND THE DRY

B\D\W\Y
BROADWAY BOOKS
New York

Copyright © 2013 by Lawrence Osborne

All rights reserved.

Published in the United States by Broadway Books, an imprint of the
Crown Publishing Group, a division of Random House LLC, a Penguin
Random House Company, New York.
www.crownpublishing.com

BROADWAY BOOKS and its logo, B \ D \ W \ Y, are registered trademarks
of Random House LLC.

Originally published in hardcover in the United States by Crown
Publishers, an imprint of the Crown Publishing Group, a division of
Random House LLC, New York, in 2013.

Portions of this work were previously published in different form as
"Drinking in Islamabad" in *Playboy* (July 2010); and as "Getting a
Drink in a Civil War" in *Harper's* (March 2011).

Library of Congress Cataloging-in-Publication Data
Osborne, Lawrence, 1958–
    The wet and the dry : a drinker's journey / Lawrence Osborne.
        p.   cm.
1. Drinking customs—Cross-cultural studies. 2. Drinking of alcoholic
beverages—Cross-cultural studies. 3. Temperance—Cross-cultural
studies. I. Title.
    GT2884.O73 2012
    394.1'2—dc23   2012038224

ISBN 978-0-7704-3690-2
eBook ISBN 978-0-7704-3689-6

Book design by Elina D. Nudelman
Cover design by Cardon Webb
Cover photograph: Stefano Lunardi/Olive

First Paperback Edition

146122990

Live secretly

—EPICURUS

CONTENTS

| THE WET | AND THE DRY

Gin and Tonic

In Milan that summer, as the temperature reached almost ninety-five every day in the deserted streets and squares around my hotel, I forced myself to stop dreaming of the fjords of Norway and the ice hotels of the Arctic Circle and, gritting my teeth, went instead to the lounge where gin and tonics were served to the guests of the Town House Galleria from a moving tray equipped with buckets of ice, lemon rinds, and glass stir-sticks. I liked to go at an hour when I knew the place would be empty, and this movable bar would be for me and me alone. The tall windows would be opened an inch, the gauze curtains flapping, the flowers wilting on the restaurant tables. The drinks trolley had stoppered crystal flagons of unnamed cognac, a bowl of marinated olives, Angostura bitters, and bottles of Fernet. It was like being in a luxury hospital where, because you are paying so much, you are entitled to drink yourself to death privately. You go right ahead, because you are human and drink is sweet.

Fashion magazines stood undisturbed on the coffee table, and in the dining room next door I could hear wealthy Russians cracking open lobster claws with silver tools and commenting ignorantly upon the wines that Europe's only seven-star hotel offers to its guests. I could hear them say "Sassicaia," then slap down the list and burst out laughing. It was six hundred euros a bottle. The waiter asked me how I would like my gin and tonic. I said that I take mine three parts tonic to one part gin, Gordon's, three ice cubes, and a dash of lime rind. The tonic brand is not an issue. The drink comes with a dim music of ice cubes and a perfume that touches the nose like a smell of warmed grass. Ease returns. It is like cold steel in liquid form.

I went to the lounge at six with some regularity, even when I had to give a lecture at the Teatro Dal Verme. One night I was interviewed by a television crew and a radio station, and the gin tasted sweeter, more maddening. I fumbled my sentences until the faces around me changed, and I could sense them asking themselves "Is he one of them?" I sat there and blathered about my latest book, which I could no longer remember, and the glass shook slightly in my hand and the ice cubes rattled. The pretty girls thought it was funny.

"Do you have a special affinity for Milan?"

"I've never been here before."

"Do you always have a gin and tonic at cocktail hour?"

Laughter.

"It's part of my heritage."

They thought this was pretty quaint, especially as the glass was still shaking in the hand of a drinker.

"It's an English drink," I said. "The national drink."

They wrote it down. Centuries ago "she" was known on the streets of London as Madame Geneva, a feminine killer.

"Cut," the director muttered.

I always end up alone with a glass and a wet lip. I sat by the windows with my forty-euro drink and admired the Galleria, the ground floor of which is occupied by a mass of bars and cafés. The architect Giuseppe Mengoni, who built it, fell to his death from the glass dome two days before it was opened in 1877. The ironwork inspired the Eiffel Tower. The cafés were lit, the Prada outlet below the hotel glittering with crystal and mirror. Chinese tourists swarmed around the small mosaic image of a bull at the center of the gallery floor, taking photographs of it. I could see the men in suits on the *terrazze* with glasses of Spritz and Negroni sbagliato and neat Campari. This was collective, merry, out-in-the-open display drinking on wicker chairs, with napkins and service and ice tongs. No one was standing, and no one was falling down. No one was shouting, no one was incontinent. The Italian style of drinking is, as we all know, organized along these lines. Men sit face to face with women and talk to them at a decibel level appropriate to sexual interest. The Galleria was intended originally as a prototype of what we would now call the mall, but it was also a covered and protected space in which to eat and drink. The protocol of the *aperitivo* and the *digestivo* was perfectly suited to its echo-friendly spaces and its allegorical frescoes.

"Other countries drink to get drunk," Roland Barthes once wrote, "and this is accepted by everyone; in France, drunkenness is a consequence, never an intention. A drink is felt as the spinning out of a pleasure, not as the necessary cause of an effect which is sought: wine is not only a philter, it is also the leisurely act of drinking." The same can be said of Italians.

I sipped my watered gin, and as always happens when I "enter" into this drink (I think of drinks as elements that are entered, like bodies of water or locales), my mind tilted its way back to the past, to the England of my childhood that I no longer possessed and that no doubt no longer existed. But why it did this was a complete enigma. As teetotalers so insistently remind those of us for whom drink is the staff of life, the mind itself is a chemical body. We are fated to control it.

Many of the hotel's guests were rich Arabs, and I would sometimes see them wandering around the restaurant with their children and their masked wives looking for a table. They would pause by the balcony and peer down at the Gucci store and then over the café terraces. Their expression seemed *almost* disdainful. It is the rich Gulf Arabs who are to a great degree the bridge between Europe and the Middle East, but I had the feeling that when they looked down at the tables crowded with multicolored alcoholic beverages, they were nonplussed, aloof. Even in Dubai, where many of them might have been from, people would not openly consume such things in public, in such spectacular spaces defined by such large crowds. It was the publicness and the ease, I think, that made them wrinkle their noses for a moment and pass on, retreating to the family dinner table laden with bottles of chilled mineral water. But I am guessing.

When we see these wealthy Muslims with their families in our luxury restaurants, we think to ourselves, as likely as not, "They have the money, but they aren't free. Look at their women. Look at the bottles of chilled mineral water on their table. They can't drink."

It is unclear which offends us more, the defacing of the women with the *hijab* (the elegance of the body suggested only by perfectly painted nails or a beautiful ankle) or the soft drinks that stand in for majestic bottles of wine, the water that stands in pathetically for a decent Brunello. We think the interdictions that govern these two things, women and alcohol, are not unconnected. It might be that it is the molecules of alcohol constantly coursing through our blood system day in and day out, night after night, their effect barely noticed most of the time, that makes the occidental feel free, unfettered, and magnificently insolent. He is, to the Muslim's eye, in a state of constant but unnoticed intoxication, but to himself he is something that commands space and uses time wisely. We are drinkers from late childhood to death, rarely if ever abstinent for the week or so necessary to discharge the last traces of alcohol from our blood.

An unusual liberty. That millionaire from Abu Dhabi could never in his worst social nightmares imagine a Saturday in Bradford. Put him in Dagenham on a weekend night at eleven, and he would not know what planet he was on. When I am in London, I sometimes take the late bus back from London Fields to Old Street, an experience instantly recognizable from images of Gin Lane. Looking down at the Galleria, he would see no passed-out girls lying in their own vomit, but the cocktails at dusk would not seem like freedom to him either. He would be baffled as to why we think that they do.

A few years before, I was riding buses through Java, much of which is dry. As I moved from town to town in an endless rigmarole of packing and unpacking, sleeping and waking, I began to feel bored and restive, or rather my blood began to thin out from its alcohol high, and I began to feel lighter, more lucid, more weighed down by anxiety.

Exhausted, I stopped for a night in the religious city of Solo, otherwise known as Surakarta. Solo is where the Bali Bombers came from, the place where the fiery religious schools preach jihad against Indonesia's tourist sector. The Al Qaeda–linked Jemaah Islamiyah group bombed the JW Marriott in Jakarta twice, first in 2003 and then on July 17, 2009. The JW in Jakarta was famous for its flashy, socialite bar. Nineteen dead. In 2002 the same group detonated two bombs inside Paddy's Pub and the Sari Club in Kuta, Bali, killing 202 people. In 2005 they repeated the stunt at a food court in Kuta and at some *warungs* (small outdoor restaurants often serving beer) at a Western-frequented beach town called Jimbaran. Twenty people were killed, many by shrapnel and ball bearings packed into the explosives. The perpetrators, later executed, called it "justice."

I stayed in a small lodge and descended into the street at dusk. The atmosphere was already peculiar.

White-robed students walked about a dry city of six hundred thousand while the mosques preached over loudspeakers. I spoke a little Bahasa, so I could make out the word "unclean" in these torrents of verbal passion, and I began to wonder if it was I who was unclean. Unclean for a number of incontrovertible reasons that could not be changed. I walked to a corner and asked a group of students if there was a restaurant I could go to that might, perhaps, serve a beer.

I had paid no heed to the images of Osama bin Laden or the long cool stares from the boys in white. I asked the question crudely but innocently. As soon as I had uttered it, I was conscious of the mistake, the potentially fatal faux pas. It was too late, of course, to back up or even run. So I had to weather the little storm that was bound to come down upon me. The boys, however, surprised me. They expressed no outrage or even annoyance at the question. Instead, they did something surprising. They invited me to a café to have a coffee and "discuss" the matter. They might be able to make me see why my question was, if not absurd (given my uncleanness), then at least unnecessary if one took the longer view.

Did I not see, they argued once we were at the café, the disasters that alcohol visited upon the Western world? It was a plague, sickness of the soul. But their reasons for agreeing with the Koran's prohibition of alcohol were not merely rigid or rote; they were, I found, quite nimbly considered. The terrible thing about drink, they said gravely, agreeing with one another, was that it took one out of one's normal consciousness. It therefore falsified every human relationship, every moment of consciousness. It falsified one's relationship to God as well. One day, they mused, the government would close down all the bars, and the capital would be beautiful again. It would be purified. "But still," I suggested, "you'd like to go there before it is purified? That would be normal."

These reedy boys in their white gear shifted on the balls of their feet, and suddenly we were all staring sheepishly at the ground, where a water bug waddled between the cigarette butts and the bottle tops. Who could speak of desires in a café flooded with the light of neon rods, in hearing of the mosque loudspeakers?

Our conversation broke off right there at the critical point, but I remembered it clearly as I was drinking that night in Milan and watching the Arab families with their bottles of Perrier. I was wet while they were dry, and with those boys it had been the same. I particularly remembered that phrase "a sickness of the soul," because the more I thought it, the more I was unable to disagree with it, though nor could I agree with it.

The two states of wetness and dryness: one balances between them. Perhaps every drinker dreams of his own prohibition, and every Muslim or Christian teetotaler dreams of a drink at the end of the rainbow. One cannot say. Certainly all things are dialectical, I thought as I went walking around Solo, hoping in some dark way that I might eventually stumble across that most delightful phenomenon, a Muslim alcoholic. (I had a soft spot not just for Muslim alcoholics but for the very idea of them. A Muslim alcoholic gives me hope that the human race can be saved.)

I went through a night market where various animals were being cut up, past cafés where men sat without women, slouched at tables of soft drinks and cans of prepared tea called Tea Pot. There was an out-of-joint, off-putting delicacy about the men. They stirred glasses of litchi juice and ate off oval plastic plates with one hand, their eyes turned on the unclean foreigner. One quickly feels paranoid.

The non-Muslim among Muslims is placed inside a unique mood. There is something pure about it, something desirable, and at the same time it grates. Was it, at this moment in Solo, the knowledge that every person there was sober and always would be?

Six hundred thousand people, I kept thinking, and not a single bar. It seemed like a recipe for madness. This was where Abu Bakar Bashir ran his Al-Mukmin boardinghouse, or *pesantren*, a spiritual home of the three men executed for the Bali bombings in 2008. It was the center for Jemaah Islamiyah, Indonesia's Islamic terror network. One of those men, Imam Samudra, gave an interview to CNN just before his execution by firing squad, during which he explained in broken English that he had learned to make bombs on the Internet and that he had been correct to massacre drinkers in bars because of the deaths incurred by "commander Bush." Another of them, Amrozi, said in the same interview that the pictures of the charred bodies produced no emotion in him whatsoever. They were, he said, "Kafirs, non-Muslims." Solo was his city, and I supposed he must have known these streets well.

The unease I felt as I went farther and farther into the night markets was also the discomfort of being dry for days on end, and I remembered it well as I sat at the Milan Town House drinking my gin and tonic and other things and listening to the crowds at the tables below, the beautiful noise of drinkers massed together under a single roof. It is only when you are surrounded by teetotalers that you realize how indebted you are to the chemistries of alcohol.

The waiter came over and asked me for the umpteenth time how I liked my gin and tonic (I had decided to waltz on with Madame Geneva), and I sank into that dim music of ice cubes and that smell of frozen grass as he mixed the drink for me. Forty euros for a gin and tonic: it seemed a little stiff, and is there a *good* gin and tonic that is thirty euros better than a bad one? I swirled the ice and tipped the glass to see the oily emulsion on the liquid's surface. So much better than a Bellini or a dreaded *sgroppino,* that Venetian mix of sorbet and vodka that all the bars in Milan seemed to have that summer. The noble "g and t" is truly a *cocktail di meditazione.* A product of India and the Raj, of the British and tropical heat and its diseases (the quinine in tonic was used to treat malaria), this simple drink is the only one I can consume quickly, the only one in which the ice does not intrude and numb.

I was now so becalmed that I could not really stand up, and I contemplated—as if from afar—the possibility of an evening spent entirely seated. The Arab matriarch glanced over at me, and I could see what she was thinking. To my surprise, however, she suddenly raised her glass of water and smiled. She seemed to know that I was not quite finished yet, or even finished at all, because one can never be finished entirely. One drinks from birth to death, unthinking. I raised my gin and tonic, therefore, and said, "Inshallah." Blasphemy, certainly, but her husband didn't hear.

A Glass of Arak in Beirut

At Le Bristol, as soon as I am alone and the lights have come up, I order a vodka martini shaken and chilled with a canned olive speared on a stick—being shaken, in the Bond manner, the drink is actually less alcoholic in its effects because more of the ice passes into the concoction. I am resolutely solitary at the hotel bar at ten past six, and the international riffraff have not yet descended upon its stools. It is *l'heure du cocktail,* and I am content. The birds are still loud on Marie Curie and nearby Al Hussein, and as yet there are no hookers strolling the carpets. I have been drinking all afternoon in my room, but after a nap and a cold bath, I have subdued the outward effects, and my hand is not shaking at all. I am alone, I think to myself, on my little lake of slightly gelatinous vodka. I am alone, and no one can touch me. I am *haraam.**

---

* In Arabic there are two words, often rendered as *haram* and *haraam* in English, that are etymologically related but distinct. The former refers to a sanctuary or holy place, the latter to that which is sinful or forbidden.

I like the Bristol, which lies so close to the Druze cemetery of Beirut; I occasionally wander there if no one has picked me up or a conversation has not dragged me down. The Druze drink alcohol, and no disrespect is possible. I also like the hour of ten past six. When I touch the rim of the night's first glass at six ten, I feel like Alexander the Great, who speared his insolent friend Cleitus during a drinking party.

The Bristol's bar is half hidden in that anxious lobby where men in dubious suits eat honeyed cakes all day long. It is an exercise in discretion. The businessmen who sit here late at night do so with tact, because not all of them are Christians. In Lebanon, which is still 40 percent Christian, alcohol is legal and enjoyed widely. I sit at the end of the bar, and my second vodka martini comes down to me on its paper serviette, with the olive bobbing on the side. Salty like cold seawater at the bottom of an oyster, the drink strikes you as sinister and cool and satisfying to the nerves, because it takes a certain nerve to drink it. Out in the street, beyond the revolving glass doors, a soldier stands with an automatic weapon staring at nothing. It is truly time for a distillate. Beer and wine are for friends, but distillations are for the drinker who is alone. I sit here watching the clock, and the barman watches me in turn, and it seems we are both waiting for something to happen.

At dusk the first addicts drift into the lobby: ill-knotted ties and self-conscious Italian shoes who grow focused under the chandeliers as they head for the bar. Soon there is that syrupy commotion of the bar stirring to life as light fades out of the outer world. Subtle intoxications take over. I look over the bottles of Gordon's and Black Label and Suntory and Royal Stag, the brand names ever prevalent in the East, and then at the tongs idling in an ice bucket and the Picard ashtrays and the barman's geometric black tie. How universal in its format the bar has become. It is like a church whose outposts are governed by a few handy principles. The stool, the mirror, the glasses hanging above by their stems, the beer mats and the wallpapers that have been chosen from suppliers to morticians. Everywhere in the world these shrines have emerged, bringing blighted happiness even to the inland towns of Papua, and everywhere they exist the cult of intoxication advertises itself with jukebox music and screens filled with faraway football games and the bottled, fancy edibles all derived from the Arab alchemists and chemists who eight hundred years ago gave us *al-kohl*—a sublimation of the mineral stibnite designed to form antimony sulfide, a fine powder that was then used as an antiseptic and as an eyeliner. Was it the fineness of powdered kohl that suggested the fineness of distilled alcohol, as some lexicographers claim? Or was it the way the "spirit" of stibnite was sublimated into that powder? Either way, in these dens we spend much of our time forgetting what we are. I light a cigarette and wonder if it is still allowed—even here in Beirut—and then I melt like a raindrop into the vodka martini itself. Vodka and smoke go well together, they seem to have been conjured out of the same essence.

The Arabs drinking next to me ask me the usual questions to which the solitary traveler is routinely subjected. I say I am taking a few months off to travel and wander, drinking my way across the Islamic world to see whether I can dry myself out, cure myself of a bout of alcoholic excess. It is a personal crisis, a private curiosity. It might end up being a few years.

"*Très bien,*" they nod, with a kind of resigned disgust.

But what is the point of that?

I say I am curious to see how nondrinkers live. Perhaps they have something to teach me.

"*Vous êtes donc un alcoolique?*"

"*En quelque sorte,*" I say. "It's my nature."

Well, they say, you can get a drink in most Islamic countries. Not, of course, in Saudi Arabia. But the psychological context is going to be very different. I say that it is precisely this context that interests me. For someone who has spent his whole life submerged in alcohol, the change of context will be illuminating.

"Illuminating?" they say.

The subject is quietly dropped. It is difficult to say if they are Sunnis or Maronites or Druze, and it is even possible that they might be Shia. They think I am a fool and a fraud, or just a drinker, and they are right. Yet there is something about vodka, I think as they chatter away; there is something about vodka that makes me indifferent and supreme.

I walk down Rome when it is quiet, past Michel Chiha and on down toward the sea, which can feel like an open brightness behind the walls of houses with their weedy trees and balconies sprouting with houseplants. Omar Daouk, and then a shortcut down through Dabbous. The knot of streets behind the Radisson, where I come for a fresh watermelon juice and a pipe when the booze has wrung me out and I need a breather. There is another hotel here in Ain el Mreisseh that I sometime stay in, the musty Bay View, where one can eat hard-boiled eggs and *labneh* in the morning looking out over the sea.

Despite the presence of the Hard Rock Café and the nightclub in the ground floor of the Bay View, well known to Saudi princes, this part of the Corniche never feels oppressive to me. I come to La Plage, where there are often entertaining weddings going on in the indoor restaurant upstairs, the girls dancing in palls of smoke, and I go down the outside steps to the tables spread out on the cement jetty below. Here the waves crash against the piles, and you can see the sloping lights of the city spreading away into darkness. The foursomes with their *shish* pipes, the exhausted wedding guests recovering with a therapeutic cigar; only a tall cold Almaza beer will do here, drunk with a plate of bitter greens and a side of *moutabal*. Almaza is for those days when the vodka has accumulated too intensely. It's my cleanser, my palate refresher.

I find myself walking home with difficulty, staggering a little as I negotiate the city's hills. Ruins remain from the wars, houses still wide open to the sky, and in my altered state they seem like obstacles to understanding a city that is already baffling. I get to the top of Rome and I hear the muezzins echoing across the *quartiers*. At a corner with a lingerie store, I grip myself by one wrist and hold myself down. Do I have to walk through yet another roadblock of skeptical soldiers in this condition, destabilized and wandering with a loose eye? It is not a

walker's city despite appearances to the contrary. The drinker
when pedestrian is at a disadvantage. I clamber past the Druze
cemetery, and a soldier stops me and asks me in broken English if I need to sit down and take a rest. It is, on reflection, a
good idea. I sit on a bollard and listen to the swallows swooping
among the old cedars by the side of the road, and I realize that
I have been drinking for hours and yet I have no memory of it.
It is negative time.

Alcohol is mentioned a mere three times in the Koran, and its
use, though frowned upon, is not always explicitly forbidden.
The hostility to wine in the holy book, if stern, does not seem
especially ferocious. It is drunkenness, rather than alcohol per
se, that provokes the Prophet's ire. The first mention of wine in
the Koran's traditional chronology, in the very first *surah* known
as "The Cow," is this: "'They ask you about drinking and gam-
bling. Say: 'There is great harm in both, although they have
some benefits for the people; but their harm is far greater than
their benefit' " (2: 219). Next we have this: "O you who believe!
Draw not near unto prayer when you are drunken, till you know
that which you utter" (4 An-Nisa 43). Later (in 5 Al-Ma'idah 91),
drink is referred to as Satan's handiwork more explicitly: "O you
who believe! Strong drink and games of chance and idols and
divining arrows are only an infamy of Satan's handiwork. Leave
it aside that you may succeed."

The Hadith is another matter. But there is little certainly about
the origin of Islam's strong interdiction of alcohol. Prohibitions

can come and go. Few remember now that coffee was prohibited in Mecca and in Egypt in the sixteenth century because it was considered an intoxicant. Some suggest that the suppression of alcohol may have arisen with the Turkish Seljuk military's desire to maintain order in its troops. No one now knows, and the beginnings of the prohibition no longer much matter. Others have claimed that it is a modern reaction against rampant Westernization, where the infidels are everywhere present through their infamous Johnnie Walker and their satanic Bong vodka.

Drinking has not disappeared, even from Saudi Arabia. The *Khaleej Times,* from time to time, regales us with harrowing accounts of Saudis who are taken to hospital after having tried to use eau de toilette as a drink. In 2006 twenty citizens of the Kingdom died after bingeing on perfume. Nothing changes the fact, meanwhile, that in the Arab land of Lebanon the national drink is arak, a distillate of aniseed.

The word *arak* in its origin means "sweat" and refers to droplets of distilled wine vapors condensing on the sides of a cucurbit. The Muslim Persian poet Abu Nuwas, in the ninth century, who wrote many verses about the pleasures of wine and distilled liquors, described it as "the color of rain water but as hot inside as the ribs of a burning firebrand." So with all distillates, which are Arab in origin and which were once exported to Europe from the Islamic lands.

Arak and the vodka martini, therefore, have a common Islamic origin. They are both the color of rainwater. And how,

sitting here morosely at the bar of the Bristol, can I not think of
the fuck-you, homosexual Abu Nuwas, who appears as a character in *One Thousand and One Nights,* and the long-dead poetry
of that genre known as *khamriyyat,* "the pleasures of drinking"? The scabrous poet who mocked "ye olde Arabia" and made
the case for the cutting-edge urban life of Baghdad. Who la-
mented the sexual passivity of men and the devious sexual appetites of women. For whom a crater on the planet Mercury is
named.

I have with me in my room my copy of *Homoerotic Songs of
Old Baghdad* and *O Tribe that Loves Boys,* even though there's
not a single affordable edition of Abu Nuwas on Amazon.com.
And this despite the poet's popularity with NAMBLA, the North
American Man-Boy Love Association. For Abu Nuwas desire is
incarnated in the *saqi,* the Christian wine boy at the tavern. *A
gentle fawn passed around the cup.* And as I sip my vodka martini in the Bristol at midnight, alone but for a bowl of salted
peanuts, those words come down through the centuries, from
the debauched salons of Baghdad.

A gentle fawn passed around the cup.
He glided among us and made us drunk,
And we slept, but as the cock was about to crow
I made for him, my garments trailing, my ram ready for
   butting.
When I plunged my spear into him
He awoke as a wounded man awakes from his wounds.
"You were an easy kill," said I, "so let's have no reproaches."

I recall that in Abu Nuwas's day, Baghdad was a city of hundreds of wineshops, just as ninth-century Muslim Córdoba must have been. Abu Nuwas saw himself as a pleasure "mine" with men and women both chipping away at his "seams":

Come right in, boys. I'm a mine of luxury—dig me.
Well-aged brilliant wines made by monks in a monastery
Shish-kebabs! Roast chickens! Eat, drink, get happy!
And afterwards you can take turns shampooing my tool.

In the early morning I drove two hours from Beirut to the Roman city of Baalbek with Michael Karam, Lebanon's preeminent wine critic. He is from an old Maronite family of Mount Lebanon, educated in England, fashioned by a disastrous spell in the British Army, a connoisseur of arak as well as of wine.

The temple lies at the head of the Bekaa Valley in Hezbollah territory, to one side of a clean little town of the same name. We sat in a café in the sun just by the ruins drinking pomegranate juice and watching black-clad clerics walk past as if they were ruminating on that morning's unpleasant electricity bills. The loudspeakers were active here. Sermons delivered at an emphatic clip. It seemed like a reasonably oppressive place, clean and safe. The kind of place where you might be kidnapped for an hour or two just to satisfy someone's curiosity. Halfway through our drink I knocked over my glass of pomegranate juice, and it fell to the ground, smashing loudly into a hundred pieces. The passersby froze for a split second. The loudspeakers started

up again, and suddenly the Roman architraves visible over the
trees seemed yearningly alien and lost. We walked over to them
with a silent, mutual relief. To step from twenty-first-century
Baalbek to first-century Baalbek felt like a blessing. The latter
was called Heliopolis. The gods that once ruled here stand facing their conqueror, divided by a parking lot.

Baal, Jupiter, Venus, and Bacchus. The Temple of Jupiter is unlike any other extant Roman building. Its scale is immense. Six
of its columns remain—the Emperor Justinian hauled off nine
for the Hagia Sophia in Constantinople; the rest were toppled by
earthquakes. Their drums lie around the pavement below. But
even these six columns quell any modern hubris. Below them
lies the Temple of Bacchus, raised by Antoninus Pius in the second century, the largest sanctuary to the wine god ever built. It
is also virtually intact, the most perfect of all buildings surviv-
ing from the Roman Empire except the Pantheon in Rome and
the remains of Ephesus the Maison Carrée in Nîmes. No one
remembers that Dionysianism was the most popular religion of
the late empire before the arrival of Christianity. It was Christianity's principal rival. Here a stoned Rasta sat on one of the
drums waving to everyone. We asked him where he had come
from. "Outer space," he said.

The cult of Venus at Heliopolis was so wild, it had to be cur-
tailed by Christian emperors. The cult of Bacchus must have
been as fierce. We walked into its temple as the sun was declining, and we could look up and see the near-perfect fretwork of
the ceilings over the outer columns. Two and a half centuries
ago they inspired the English architect Robert Adam in his

decor at Osterley House in Hounslow. We went into the *cella*, which felt like the nave of a church, still partially roofed, the niche carvings still preserved, the steps to the altar intact. One rarely thinks of the cult of Dionysus-Bacchus having an actual church and a rite that may have influenced Christianity very early on. Scholars like Carl Kerényi have argued that the figure of Christ absorbed many of the characteristics of Dionysus. But here you suddenly become aware of this possibility.

I sat on the steps and listened to the echoing Hezbollah sermons coming from the town. I could sense that Michael was thinking the same thing. I glanced down at the marble relief at the foot of the steps and saw a single panel with a dancing girl etched into it, pristinely chiseled, her hair and chiton flowing. A bacchante from the time of Antoninus Pius. She was no bigger than my hand, so tiny perhaps she had been forgotten by all the looters. Like the sculpted girls you can see in remote Angkorian temples in Cambodia, she had survived against the odds. A follower of Bacchus caught in a single moment and still here, spinning to her god's energy.

Nowhere else does the transitory nature of religions seem so obvious. They seem fixed and immovable, but they are not. They are constantly receding and re-forming and fragmenting into pieces. Thus they are always prey to paranoia, because they know that they are far more transitory than they can afford to admit. We have even forgotten that Dionysianism was a religion at all.

Yet the energy of cults passes on into the new cults that replace them. I put my palm over the marble girl and closed my eyes. One has to remember what she was dancing to, and why intoxication is the most primitive mystery. In the Mediterranean world, it was at the origin of a religious passion. Today we have turned that same passion into a secular industry and a private struggle. But meanwhile Hezbollah are right to hate the drinker: he, and this delicate marble girl, are their greatest threat.

Fear and Loathing in the Bekaa

On the coast a few miles north of Beirut lies the port of Batroun. Its name comes from the Greek for grape, *botrys,* which suggests it was one of the great wine ports of the ancient world. In the sun and the smell of thyme, in the dust of hills that seem to turn to powder every time the sea wind hits them, I was driving to Batroun with Michael Karam again. We drove along the edge of a forest fire, towering dark-orange flames rising above the silhouettes of cedars. But the villages nevertheless had a soft luminosity, paths carved between vineyards and fields of sunflowers.

Just as Mount Lebanon, Michael says, imparts a mysterious atmosphere of rain and mist and melancholy to the wines that are made there—like Château Musar—so this coast pours its pagan brightness and heat into juices. A land drenched by sea light, the hills of Kfifane, Edde, and Jrane.

We were driving to Coteaux de Botrys, a winery founded ten years ago by a retired Lebanese general named Joseph G. Bitar.

Bitar left it to his daughter Neila. Neila is a famous beauty. A redhead who sleeps with a loaded pistol under her pillow. After a long exile in Germany, she came back to Lebanon, like so many others. War drove this middle class away, and stability and yearning for home brought them back. They brought with them Europe's alcoholic tastes, which were then grafted onto Lebanon's own traditions—these are Christian families, and wine and arak are woven into their sense of self. Wine is sacral to the Maronites. But whereas they left the country as a slight majority, they have returned as a minority. The Muslim birthrate is higher, and the Christian grip on power has melted away.

It is the Christians who have created Lebanon's new food and wine culture, selling their wines to the critics who fly in from the occidental metropolises, creating the "organic" eateries that serve as the frame. It is they who are drawing this country of the Middle East back toward European Epicureanism, with all the money and media voyeurism that go with it. As the only Arab country with a wine culture, it must be the bridge between those two entities canonized as East and West but that could also be called Wet and Dry, Alcoholic and Prohibited.

On either side of the small road, we soon saw the sloping vines of Coteaux de Botrys shining despite a pall of smoke, and the valley that falls down to the cranes and the construction dust of Batroun and the blue line of the sea. Wealthy villas crowned the hilltops. The redhead was already there in slippers, holding a bottle of Cuvée de l'Ange. The winery is just a house with a terrace, and Neila is a general's daughter with a taste for grenache.

She had made a lunch with chicken stewed in beer. The

terrace looked over the valley of vines, and on the far side rose the country mansion of Beirut's largest car salesman. It looked like a maximum-security prison surrounded by electric fences and arc lamps. We drank the Cuvée de l'Ange, a mix of Syrah, Mourvèdre, and grenache, and listened to the aerial echo of Israeli warplanes, which have right of passage over the whole country. Neila told me why she wanted to come back to Lebanon and make wine. There was something frail and watchful about her, a grimly delicate humor that waited to reveal itself. Her wine goes to the head. Michael also, as it happens, is a child of exile—his Lebanese father and Egyptian mother took their children to London to escape the civil war, and he returned only in the nineties, his Arabic almost forgotten. He had to learn his own language all over again. Yet his political roots in Lebanon are profound. His grandmother was early on involved in the Syrian National Party, which in the 1930s advocated the union of Lebanon and Syria, before it became quasi-fascist in recent years; his father's family is old Mount Lebanon.

Both of them burn with an idea of what the future of the country might hold if a cosmopolitan and bibulous spirit were to become entrenched. Drink becomes the wedge of freedom in a land otherwise haunted by the religious men in black. So they looked down at Batroun, and Neila said, "It's Greek and Phoenician, like us. Someone told me once that Dionysus set off for Greece from here. He went with the wine ships that traded with Attica."

Dionysus might have been a Phoenician god originally from these mountains, exported through places like Botrys; a god whom the Greeks regarded as an import from the East and

whose earliest festivals were rooted in the Attic wine ports. But
he was a dead god here now. The god of the desert was now in
the ascendant once again.

With a papaya tart we drank Neila's arak Kfifane, made from
aniseed and *merweh* grape and distilled five times, and I asked
her why she slept with a gun under her head.

"The goats, they eat the grapes. I shoot them."

But also one never knows who will come out of those beautiful hills. A wine critic or a man with a Kalashnikov.

Parts of the Bekaa are modeling themselves on Napa or
Bordeaux—the tourist seduction, the country inns, the twee
foodie experiences. The wet and the dry, as it were, side by side
in a spirit of mutual incomprehension, as in those counties in
Texas where you can buy a beer in one and yet not drink it in
the next one along. "I've heard," Michael said, "you have to put
a bottle of wine inside a paper bag when traveling on the New
York subway. Is that true?" Naturally it is. On the street, in the
subway, in a park. It is the same principle as the Victorians covering their piano legs. It would be unimaginable in Arab Beirut
outside of Shia neighborhoods like Dahiya.

I said I had also noticed that Beirut had more lingerie stores
than New York, and better ones, too. And for that matter Gemmayze had wilder bars than the Brooklyn I lived in. Each society engages in its own war on pleasure. The American war on
pleasure is more total, perhaps, more earnest, because Lebanon
in the end is a Mediterranean place, Greek and Phoenician as its
people are always reminding you, as well as Arab. A glimpse of
the Arabs as they would be without Islam.

I recalled a political meeting I went to in Dahiya with some moderate Shia clerics. It was held in a community center at night, the doors watched by armed guards, and someone had asked the clerics if they thought their moderation would ever extend to allowing a bar to open in that neighborhood. It was intended as a humorous aside, and the clerics smiled along, stroking their nicely tailored beards and understanding that such questions are merely provocative. The answer was no.

At nightfall we went to Abdel Wahab in Ashrafieh on the street of that name, Abdel Wahab El Inglizi, named it is sometimes thought for some Englishman or other passing through Beirut. The restaurant has an upper terrace open to the sky, the tables widely spaced and filled with large parties at their ease. We ordered little sausages, *fatoosh, moutabal,* and *labneh* and a bottle of Le Brun from the Domaine des Tourelles in the Bekaa, considered by many the greatest arak of the Middle East.

A distilled rather than a fermented drink can be an experience of being "out of time," and yet it does not obscure the past. A fermentation excites and fills one with optimism and lust; a distillation makes one morose, skeptical, and withdrawn.

We drank this Le Brun, and the latter feelings began to arise. But with them came a detachment, a sense of distance from the self that was refreshing. There was in this drink, also, a strong sense of place. Not just of Lebanon but of the Bekaa Valley where it was made. It came from the country's oldest winery and distillery. Drinking it was not frivolous or carefree. It was like entering a church.

.   .   .

When the French engineer François-Eugène Brun came to the Bekaa Valley in 1868 to lay down the Damascus-to-Beirut railway for an Ottoman company, he found a Christian land worked by monks. Modest and probably thorny wines were made in the remote monasteries of the valley, and Brun decided to stay and make his own variation of them. Wines for the sacrament in the churches of Damascus and Beirut. The difference was that he intended to sell it in the cities. So was born Lebanon's first commercial wine, and Brun's descendants by marriage and inheritance still work the tiny Domaine des Tourelles, off the main road that runs through the farming town of Chtaura two hours from Beirut. The next day I went there.

After the last actual Brun, Pierre-Louis, died in 2000, the winery was bought by Nayla Kanaan Issa-el-Khoury and Elie Issa, descendants of the original Brun's Lebanese wife. I was met by Christiane Issa, their daughter, who runs the company's PR, and it is she who took me through the nineteenth-century warrens of little rooms stuffed with decayed Christ pictures and sacks of green aniseed with their grassy perfume and the tasting rooms with their shelves of Orangine and Brou de Noix and dusty wine medals from the 1930s. The Coq compressors from Aix looked as ancient as water wheels, and through the windows I could see the scarfed Shia girls walking between the walls and glancing over into the arak distillery, which is *haraam*, with a look in the eye that is difficult to define.

Since the Bekaa is Hezbollah's stronghold, it is not impossible that one day the Valley will stop making wine altogether. Christiane entertained this dark idea with a kind of apocalyptic relish.

"Think of the birthrates. They are out-breeding us."

"Who are?"

"The Muslims. We can't keep up. The Bekaa will soon be all Shia. We'll be switching to fruit juice production."

"Is it possible?"

"It is possible. What if they just said, No more alcohol?"

She opened her hands wide.

After the visit I walked out into the main road of Chtaura, thick with the farm dust of passing tractors and the pickups racing to the Syrian border. The town cowers under jagged peaks that belittle its efforts at homeliness and business. It seems like a menaced desert frontier.

Down the hill were a few *shawarma* restaurants with cars parked outside, loud, family-fun places with ovens and grills. On the way to one of these, I saw a shop where I could buy a can of beer. Since I was parched and could not contemplate opening the two bottles of arak I was carrying, I stepped in, bought the beer, and walked on to the largest of the *shawarma* places, which was called Ikhlass.

I noticed at once that the mood was not entirely normal. It was possible, after all, that my two bottles of arak and can of beer had been spotted at once, even though they were legal. The glass doors were guarded by a small posse of the men in shades whom one learns in this part of the world to give a wide berth to. But now they could not be avoided. I went up to the outdoor grill and got the *shawarma*. The men in shades rotated toward

me, distastefully curious. There was something going on inside
the restaurant. It was a prominent Hezbollah cleric in for his
lunchtime *shawarma*. The men in shades stared at my beer and
I asked the grill master if I could sit inside and drink it with my
shawarma. Sure, he said. You can drink that stuff if you have
to. Since there was nowhere else to go but the street, I went into
the restaurant past the scowling guards and sat as far away as
I could from the dining cleric. It was, in fact, the staff who appeared most jarred. The men around the cleric, for their part,
appeared merely contemptuous. The cleric turned for a moment
and looked at me. A conversation, I thought hopefully. But there
was no chance of that. Their eyes alighted upon the frothing
can of beer, and in them was a sort of hardened pity, as if I and
my can did not really exist in this world.

I went to Château Massaya and had lunch with the winemaker
Ramzi Ghosn. He insisted that Hezbollah was not a problem.
Their people made substantial earnings as vineyard workers,
and in the light of this reality the clerics would turn a blind eye.
Shiites always cut a deal. It was the Sunni fanatics who were the
darkest version of the future.

"The boys with beards up in the hills, they are the ones who
make me sleepless at night. They are the madmen. The Shia are
something else."

"Not true fanatics?"

"Not about these things."

Halfway through lunch two German tourists arrived. They

were "mobile publishers." They had just brought out a biography of Khalil Gibran and were sailing around Lebanon by themselves in a minivan filled with their books, which they hoped to sell in towns and villages across the land. They were hearty, sensitive, and sandaled—in short, everything I loathe—but the man with his graying mustache and vivid eyes was a true scholar of Lebanese wine. He could list them all, literally, and then he could provide each name with an instantly recalled tasting note. It was a feat of memory and also of devotion, of love for a culture in which he was, in the end, a superfluous visitor.

"Oh, we love Lebanon," they kept saying, nodding sadly, as if it were a mystery even to themselves.

They joined us and we drank some of the house Massaya. It was serviceable wine and went well with the lamb chops, the *labneh*, the fresh mint. I was sure that the conversation would now settle into the usual babble of gastronomes and foodies, but as we were about to talk about wine, there was a distant overhead rumble, and Ramzi said, quite laconically, as if the following observation were not even worth making, "It's the Israeli air force. We are a country that cannot even control its own skies."

The Germans tutted over Israel.

"You see?" the wine scholar said. "Now you know why Hezbollah has such a following."

"Between Israel and Hezbollah," the lady said. "Poor Lebanon."

Ramzi now rose nationalistically to the occasion.

"We are surrounded by more powerful countries. Yes. But none of them have our joie de vivre, our way of life, our wine"—he fumbled a little—"our women, our—our—well, our lamb chops. Have you ever eaten a better lamb chop in the Middle East?"

"Never."

"There is nothing in the Middle East like us. Where else can you drink wine?"

"Israel," I said.

There were exasperated shrugs.

Did I know, Ramzi continued, that the Bekaa Valley was the northern tip of the Rift Valley that extended all the way to Kenya and was the birthplace of the human race?

"What a dreadful idea," I said, "that the human race had a birthplace."

After an apple dessert, to catch the dusk, I made my way a few miles into the valley to the Umayyad ruins of Anjar, a bleak and lonely place at sundown.

The Arab city was abandoned in the eighth century, though no one knows why. The ruins today are encircled by a long wall, outside which lies a shabby village populated with resettled Armenians. The signs are all in Armenian, but the Syrian secret police maintain a heavy presence—they ran Lebanon from this unnoticed backwater for many years. An atmosphere of physical fear oozes from the empty roads, and the elegant, pencil-thin vaults and arches of the Umayyad architects stand in cool isolation.

As I walked up the main flagged road, I sensed that the columns on either side were actually Byzantine, looted from another site perhaps, and at the ancient city's main crossroads huge Roman columns rose out of classical pediments scored with Greek graffiti. It is the language of power, too, but expressed in porphyry.

The Umayyad elegance stands side by side with this more powerful and more ancient form, uneasy, envious, and imitative but reaching out for a definition of its own. I sympathize with those newly arrived Arabs of the seventh century, a desert people obsessed with water wandering into a land of vines where the peasants still cried "Dionysus!" at harvest time. When the *inglizi* got lost, however, in the dark mazes of the past, the armed guards came to look for him with torches. They called "Hey, Tommy!" into the abandoned bathhouses and mosque, alarmed that the Syrians might suspect that he was up to no good, whereas in reality the suspicion was merely that he was drunk and good for nothing, not even for finding his way home.

Lunch with Walid Jumblatt

Beirut for me is like Naples, a
place that tears up the stable personality of the visitor. The
crime and lassitude, the beauty, the intense melodrama of the
street, the melancholy sea; the bars where life seems to stop and
then begin again and then stop again. Bars in a city that is half
Muslim are like brothels in a city that is Catholic, and the Beirut bar has an innocent intensity all its own. Though come to
think of it, Catholic cities are excellent places to find brothels.

One night I might favor Grey Goose in Ashrafieh, and another
night the rooftop bar of the Albergo Hotel on Abdel Wahab El
Inglizi, that French Mandate street of shutters and cloistered
gardens and multimillion-dollar condos and long strolls after
dinner. The Albergo, in fact, is one of the bars I have written
down in my Black Book of Bars in case, in an inebriated fit, I
forget its address. A tall hotel in Belle Epoque style, it has an
ironwork elevator, a beautiful and secretive bar on the ground
floor, and another one on the roof laid out under shades and

with views over the city's lights. One can even drink on the floor below, inside the restaurant, where gin and tonics are served at sofas so deep that the drinker disappears into them like stones sinking into quicksand. But there are so many bars in this febrile city; in Gemmayze you can spend entire nights wandering through them, unable to count them or hold them to account. I have not even mentioned the Couqley in its alleyway, where I came with Michael to eat oysters with Entre Deux Mers and steaks *saignants* with bottles of Hochar red, a restaurant where one can drink all afternoon and into the evening and then into the small hours in the same way that you would smoke a pipe all the way down over the course of a day. And there are bars I have forgotten, name-wise, though I remember their dedication—touching and sincere—to a single prewar cocktail. One night at a bar opening by the fashion designer Johnny Farah in the port, Farah served us a Trinity, a kind of dinosaur dry martini that was reputed to be the distant origin of the more famous concoction. It's a perfect three-way split between sweet and dry vermouth and gin, but here it was complemented by intense Beirut lemon zest and drops of orange bitters. Rich and clear, with an acidic sweetness, it has none of the formidably "grown-up" sourness of the dry martini, yet it's not sickly. In Christian Beirut, its name no doubt has its own "feel."

Beirut is the only city where the bar and muezzin cannot dominate each other. From Abdel Wahab, Furn El Hayek runs gently downhill toward Saints Coeurs, past Ottoman houses with their balconies and high arches intact, the gardens dark with hundred-foot trees. Near the bottom, on St. Joseph University

Street, stands Time Out, which may be the oldest continuously running bar in Beirut. It is built into three floors of a house that was once a *table d'hôte* in the late nineteenth century and is now like an English country home with a basement of white stone vaults. Here is that perfect bar: a worn-in room with, at its center, a great wall of bottles in niches, and around it armchairs and oils and shaded lamps and, leaning on said bar, the white-haired and bearded Jacques Tabet, who during the civil war was known cryptically as Beirut Number Three. Tabet is Beirut's most cantankerous and generous bar owner, and his creation is very like himself: interconnected rooms like salons in a private house, an unlit garden terrace, corners where men can smoke cigars without occidental disapproval. A bar for adults, in other words, and not for screaming children. In New York it would have been closed down long ago for this very reason.

During the war the bar was hit numerous times by RPGs and small-arms fire. "Small ordnance," as Tabet says, "because the people shooting at us were right next door." Survival is part of its charm. "I hate being sober," he continues, pouring me seven or eight red ports. "It's a state that irritates me, as I am sure it irritates you. If I had been sober all these years, I would not have survived." And downstairs in the basement of this house, which used to belong to Tabet's great-grandparents, one finds Beirut's most famous bartender, Johnny Khouris. To Khouris one must come when one needs a proper dry martini in Beirut. No one else's will do. And so nights can pass under the chipped stone vaults that look as if they are made of chalk, among the house cats and the men who have that distant war still in their faces and in their gestures. Is alcohol, I wonder as I sit there, a substance that separates the consciousness from its true self and therefore from others? If that is true, then we spend our entire lives in a state of subtle falsity. But is alcohol the creator of the mask, or the thing that strips it away?

There are moments, as I sit at a bar in some forlorn neighborhood, whether it be here in Beirut or elsewhere, alone usually and distanced from the human race as if by a stone wall, when I can hear something trickling deep inside my core, like a sound of dirty water moving through a wood, and it seems to me that I am living in slow motion. The fingers close around the glass in slow motion; the ice cubes shift in slow motion; the images in the mirrors around me are frozen. I have entered a sedentary state of suspended animation, my mouth moving and words coming out, but having nothing to do with me. I am a puppet, but the subtlety and charm of puppets should never be underestimated.

When I meet another drinker at the bar, it is like two puppets bowing to each other and then fencing. But usually, as I say, I am alone, and it is this quality of aloneness that is most special. The solitude of the bar is so absolute, so gutting that you wonder why Edward Hopper didn't paint it more often. It is a place where social leprosy is normal; Islam, whose traditional cities are communitarian and domestic, sees no need for such isolation at the altar of Johnnie Walker. But there are sects within Islam, like the Druze, where alcohol is permitted—what of them?

. . .

I had lunch one of those days of Beirut spring with the Druze warlord Walid Jumblatt in the Shuf Mountains. I remembered Jumblatt from my school days during the Lebanese civil war of the 1970s, with his ruthless militia, his love of motorbikes, and his leather jackets. He was a legendary figure, a chilling figure. A killer, an ethnic cleanser, a man whose own father had been assassinated by the Syrians; but at the same time a man of the world, a sophisticate, a playboy familiar with Antibes and BMW bikes.

The idea of meeting him in the flesh thirty-five years on was startling. It was on a press visit offered by Saad Hariri, prime-minister-to-be at that moment, and leader of the March 14th reform movement. It was going to be a lunch full of bonhomie and political sympathy, with Jumblatt frail in his corduroys, the aristocratic grandson of the great pan-Arabist Prince Shakib Arslan, his famous bald pate ringed with white hair: a deceptive, soft-spoken mignon who knew how to charm.

In his dining room decorated with scabbarded swords and bucklers, the questions put to Jumblatt were about Hezbollah and Syria, his future relations with them. He is the leader of the PSP Socialist party, and he is expected to hold positions of interest to American scribes. He listened and talked, holding forth. The conversation was enjoyable. The windows were open, and we could smell the snow. On the table was a bottle of Château Kefraya, the wine that Jumblatt invests in. As I was seated next to him, he politely poured me a glass. The politics died down, and he seemed genuinely curious to hear what a drinker would think of his production. Jumblatt has owned the winery since the late 1980s, and for some fifteen years now his wine has been one of the most popular in Lebanon. It's a thick, juicy American-ized wine, more or less revolting, and I said it was wonderful—it didn't seem wise to brandish conflictual tasting notes with a vigneron warlord. The warlord and winemaker seemed like two incompatible personalities converged by fate into a single human frame that might barely be able to hold them together.

"Good," he said. "I'll send a magnum to your hotel room."

My heart sank. My goose was cooked because however bad it was, I knew that, once locked in my room, I would drink the whole thing in an afternoon. Walid himself did not drink, how-ever. I asked him how it was that the Druze, who are Muslims of a sort, do so.

"It's because we do not follow sharia. We pray three times a day and not five. When we say 'jihad,' we mean something very different from war against outsiders. A war against oneself."

The Druze are mysterious to others. The writer Benjamin of Tudela described them in 1165 as "mountain people, monothe-ists, who believe in the eternity of the soul and in reincarnation." They are derived from a sect of Ismaili Shiites who founded the sect in Cairo under the Shia Fatimids. Al-Darzi, the preacher for whom they are named, was Persian. They advocated the abo-lition of slavery and a more mystical, depoliticized Islam that borrowed much from Greek and Persian traditions. Estranged even from other Shiites, they are denounced outright by Sunnis. They drink, but they are forbidden to eat watercress.

I wanted to ask him not about Israel or Hezbollah but about Al-Hakim, the mad imam and ruler of the Fatimids from 996 to 1021, who the early Druze of Cairo thought was an incarnation of God. I wanted to ask him if any scholar knows what Al-Hakim's policy on alcohol was. But the question seemed oddly impertinent, and I knew full well that almost no one can unravel the mystical threads of the Ismaili.

So I asked him instead about his vineyards in the Bekaa Valley.

"The Bekaa is dominated by Hezbollah now. And I am sure one day they will cut the water to the vineyards. Well, I say they might do it, not that they will. They can't make Lebanon dry, but they can make it drier."

He watched me drink with a shrewd looseness, his head slightly tilted, and asked me again if I thought Kefraya was a wine that could do well in America. It was, to me, a wine crafted with precisely that in mind. "Good, good," he said.

When the meal was over, we moved to arak. He was pleased that we liked Château Kefraya and his own arak, and that we seemed to understand that his country was made of shifting sands, and that one day he might condemn the teetotalers in black on the far side of the hills and the next year join forces with them to survive.

"And you," he said, "you seem to like your wine. How do you find our arak?"

"It's like ouzo, only better."

"The Greeks took it from us, not the other way around. Arak is the soul of Lebanon. Another one?"

I was already a little slow.

"I am half Irish," I said. "It's best not to get me drinking at two o'clock in the afternoon. The genes."

I felt the slight panic even now as my hand was curled around a tiny glass of arak, and the old man's eyes were on that hand as well. It was as if this shrewd observer of human nature had suddenly detected the flaw in my person, which was not even a very well-disguised flaw. The arak gave off a slightly juicy fragrance, and its clarity made it seem innocuous.

After lunch we toured the grounds. Jumblatt's castle is landscaped with cypresses and rosebushes and the Roman sarcophagi that he likes to collect. A greyhound loped silently alongside as we were shown the grounds. He took us into his designer library, filled with his father's Soviet memorabilia. The Jumblatts were Soviet allies during the civil war, and Brezhnev sent Walid's father, Kamal, this life-size oil of Marshal Zhukov astride a white horse, as well as some lovely military pistols that are now displayed on Walid's desk. A splendid library with a fine collection of *La Nouvelle Revue Française.*

"Yes," he said fondly. "How glamorous Communism seemed in those days. How inevitable."

"Did Khrushchev," I asked, "send any rare vodka over?"

"I can't recall. He may have."

I walked out into the gardens and looked at the tombs with their stone garlands and putti and I saw the snowlines of the Shuf through the cypresses. I was still vibrating from the wine and the arak, and I could not hold my senses still. *The landscape seen through arak,* I thought. Luminous and reposed and near. Distilled, you might say. Clarified and intensified to the point of serene madness.

The Ally Pally

In Abu Dhabi, I awoke late in the afternoon in the Fairmont Bab al Bahr. I was in the same clothes that I had been wearing for weeks in Beirut, and with a headache so severe that I had to lie there for some time and try to remember where I had been the night before. It is curious to wake up fully clothed, and my clothes were wet. I was in a suit with cufflinks attached, a tie askew, slip-ons with no socks. I was dressed, in other words, for a late-night party of moderate but not quite serious elegance. There was a bowl of fruit by the bed with a banana and a star anise and, next to them, a tray of handmade chocolates. Nothing had been touched.

I sat in my room on the eighth floor of the Bab al Bahr as the sun was declining. A thin moon had appeared over the waterway that separated the hotel's artificial beach from the cranes and silos on the far side. There, in a fluctuating light, stood the world's eighth-biggest mosque, eighty-two Mogul-inspired Bianco marble domes clustered together and framed by virtually every window in the largely glass-covered Fairmont. The Sheikh Zayed Grand Mosque can accommodate forty thousand worshippers and houses the world's largest carpet as well as the world's largest Swarovski chandelier. Being the Emirates, this quality of being the largest and tallest and grandest is important.

One is supposed to know these things and to apply them in one's mind to the buildings themselves as one looks at them. Even from the futuristic lobby of the Fairmont, where the architecture is opulently immanent, the metal and glass columns changing color every few seconds, the boldness of the mosque was arresting as it was seen through the back windows. The piety of the Emirates' capital is often underrated. Even in that lobby, surrounded by partying princes and Western girls in Pucci skirts, the fact that I was no longer in a city of wine and sea was obvious. The desert and its faith had replaced it.

The Fairmont bar was called Chameleon. Two guys shook the mixers like Mexican rattles, and by midnight *le tout Abu Dhabi* was at its counter shouting for things mostly made with vodka and various fruit juices. The drinking was intense, and it was an Arab crowd, if not necessarily an Emirati one. The bar glittered with Absolut and Grey Goose and Bong and Cape North and Stoli elit.

The most humbling thing about drinking is the instantaneous erosion of recent memory. As the mind reassembles itself after a poisoning, it is full of questions, but it finds no answers. The hangover burned on. I couldn't remember how I had ended up.

I gazed down at an artificial beach, at a long pool surrounded by sun beds and dark blue towels. I had been at the opening of this very bar the night before, but I had been carried home by the staff—carried or hustled or encouraged, I couldn't say—and laid to rest in my executive suite bed like a pensioner who has collapsed at a bus stop. A hangover is, moreover, a complex thing. It is slow, meditative; it inclines us to introspection and clarity. The aftereffect of a mild envenoming is cleansing mentally. It enables one to seize one's mind anew, to build it up again and regain some kind of eccentric courage.

When I was a child, I remember being puzzled by the hangovers of adults, which I had many opportunities to observe close up. My parents staggered about silently, holding on to things to steady themselves, and their speech was unusually gentle. They seemed ghostlike in this state, and I preferred them that way. They had slowed down, and it made them seem like robots, or at least they reminded me that the human body is a machine after all and that it can be impaired easily.

Watching them, I could not help but be aware that if this was the effect of their drug of choice, this same drug could well end up being mine. Furthermore, it was curious that in a middle-class England that preached so much about the virtues of being sober, and therefore industrious, the adults who sustained this culture and bore such responsibility for it should spend so much time lumbering about completely stoned.

The telephone rang by the bath later that night. I was almost asleep, dreaming sadly about these matters, as we all do when the house of our parents has been destroyed and scattered to the winds, and I had trouble making words connect. It was long distance, which inevitably meant America. Chirpy tones, anxiety, and somebody wanting something.

"Hi, it's Jen from the *Faster Beast*! Are you having breakfast? I wanted to catch you—"

"Before I got up?"

"If only. By the way, you *are* up early. That's not like you. How's the sun?"

"Shining."

"They told me there's a really cool view of the mosque. It's an awesome hotel, isn't it? Did you go to the opening of Chameleon last night? It would be great if you could file it by tonight your time. Or even this afternoon. Or even earlier."

"Why not right now?"

"Could you? The editor wants to know what new cocktail trends are making waves in the Arab world. You know, cool bartenders, exciting new trends—ah—new formulas for the Arab Revolution, and that sort of thing. Like, where are the kids going for their sundowners after they've been protesting all day?"

"Liz, I have to go. There's a large lizard in my bath."

"Jen. It's Jen."

"I'll file tonight, Jen. Thanks for getting me on the executive floor, by the way."

"Oh, no problem."

The irritation in the distant voice could hardly control itself.

"So what did you drink?" she asked testily.

"A thing called the Arabian Night."

"Cool. Was it a girl drink? Was it postgender?"

"It was vermouth, Worcestershire sauce, vodka, sugar, crab-apple juice, lime, Angostura bitters, seltzer water, lemonade, champagne, a twist of grapefruit, and Coke."

"Oh."

"I drank it with the sundown. It made me violent."

"Did you go to a protest?"

I went downstairs at noon and sat in the buffet restaurant on the ground floor, which is quite an Abu Dhabi social scene. It is one of those buffets learned from the great hotels of the East. Multi-ethnic, sophisticated, generous in scope and quality. A manifestation of the new middle-class culture that girdles the world and that enjoys its lunches with little reference to any specific Western origin. The women were veiled but wore mall jewelry of the highest order. Their hands were heavily tattooed in the desert way, but the shoes were Forzieri. The men sat together in groups outside, their children darting among them, in an ambience of wealth and relaxation. A self-conscious participation in modern family hedonism.

The cuisines of the buffet were Gulf Arab, Lebanese, Japanese, Egyptian, Italian, and Indian, with a few dabs of English—baked beans and link sausages and squares of fat-drenched toast. There were counters of tropical fruits; juice bars that liquefied kiwis and mangoes on the spot. Dessert isles with dozens of handmade mousse fondants and *îles flottantes* and strawberry *kulfi*. One could discreetly order a glass of wine, but as one did so, there would be a subtle inspection by the server, an instantaneous assessment of one's background religion.

If you were Muslim, you would be declined, I imagine. If you were Jewish, you would be thrown out, and if you were

Christian, you would be allowed a drink. I am not saying this is the hotel's policy, of course. Tall green cocktails indeed made the rounds, but what was in them? In any case, I ordered a Diet Coke to mix up my gourmet *fuul* and behind my sunglasses tried to eat and Coke my way out of the lingering brain fog, as I call my hangovers. The mists within began to part. I got up, finally, and walked through the glass doors out into the suffocating sunshine, my balance only slightly akilter, my ears ringing. I walked past the pool, where the chubby white girls lay sweating in oil like things slowly simmering in pan fat.

There were two breakwaters of piled stones and an artificial beach between them, and across the water the cranes shone in a pall of dust. I stood on a breakwater and watched the Coast Guard launches trawl by. The day was already way past ninety degrees, and the sky was beginning to haze. All the controlled, anal emptiness of Abu Dhabi was concentrated in this single view dominated by the world's biggest mosque. I had suddenly forgotten, in some sense, who I was as I waved to the Coast Guard, and why I was. I should have remembered, but someone remembered for me, because as I dropped onto the beach and walked along it, a man from the deck chairs rose, dusted himself down, and came toward me. He raised his hand, called "John!" in an English voice, and came down onto the sand. He was, oddly, dressed for a business meeting, though he had been sunning himself by the pool with a jungle hat. I stopped. He came plodding down, saying "Oi, John!"

He was unknown, but he seemed to know me. In that light we both looked like ghosts, almost transparent, and I knew at once what was up; I had met this loser in the bar last night and had no recollection of him, but he had easily recognized me. John, that was me. I must have called myself "John" all evening. But who was John?

"Oi, John, I knew it was you. I see you're up and about."

"I'm sorry—"

"James. From the bar."

"Yeah, James."

"John, good to see you. I thought you were dead."

Laughter.

"No, just out cold for the morning."

"My wife said you should have been dead. Eleven mai tais. Blimey. We both thought you was dead."

"Was it eleven?"

"More than that, cock. You're a right fish."

"Am I?"

"Dead right you are, mate. You passed out."

"I did? Where?"

"In the pool. Don't you remember passing out in the pool?"

A playful arm-punch and a wink. The hideous dyed hair glistened in the sun, and the oyster eyes contracted.

"Wait," I said. "I don't remember anything about a pool."

"Come on, mate. You remember the *pool*. That was the funniest thing I saw all year."

I was now sweating copiously, and we were walking.

"The pool? What did I do in the pool?"

"You don't remember doing the jackknife?"

"The jackknife?"

"Yeah, you did a jackknife into the pool. The missus said it was the funniest thing she's seen all year."

"You're kidding."

"No, mate. You're kidding. We all pissed ourselves."

Who are you? I wanted to ask.

"So I did a jackknife?" I said.

"Yeah, it was a good one. You didn't come up for five minutes."

Underwater, then. A memory of drowning bubbles, panic, and now it was coming back in little pieces. The wobbling diving plank, the sudden elevation toward the stars.

"Yeah," I muttered. "I always do a jackknife on rum."

"I believe it."

He seemed very pleased with me.

"Are you coming to the Ally Pally tonight?" he asked. "All the lads will be there. After your jackknife, I would say you have honorary admission to the Ally Pally."

"What is the Ally Pally?"

"The best bar in Abu Dhabi. You've been to the Ally Pally, surely?"

We had now entered the high-design glass cage of the hotel and were standing by Marco Pierre White's restaurant. He told me all about John, a contractor for hotel construction all over the Middle East. Married, three kids, ten years younger than me, and a decent shot at snooker. John was a sweet talker, mild mannered, and full of anecdotes about the construction business, but when he got drinking, he chased every lady in the bar. He went berserk in his quiet gentlemanly way, and there was no constraining him. He told me all this as if I needed to hear it from a third person, as if this real me were totally unknown to the person standing in front of him right then.

"And did I say anything untoward to the ladies?" I asked as we took the escalator up to the dazzling Barbarella lobby, where a few sheikhs in *ghutrahs* and rope *agal* sat on the sofas with their overdecorated wives.

"Not at all, John. You was politeness itself. But the staff had a hard time getting you out of the pool."

I must have been on a roll, I thought grimly. It happens sometimes, some switch is thrown inside me and all the controls cease to function. My Jewish male friends in New York say it never happens to them.

By now I was curious as to why he had walked up with me into the lobby, and I supposed it was because I was now an interesting specimen. The English are very indulgent to episodes of alcoholic insanity. They strike them as sympathetic, understandable, and a sign of being a real human being, however inconsequential such episodes might be.

"You come down to the Ally Pally at eight," he said in comradely fashion. "It's not as bad as they say. The Chinese hookers don't arrive till ten at the earliest. We'll have shots with the lads."

"All right," I said. "It can't be any worse than Chameleon."

"Oh, it's way above Chameleon, John. There's no darts at Chameleon, for one thing. No hookers neither."

"True enough," I agreed, shaking my head. "They wouldn't allow darts and hookers at Chameleon."

"And what's a bar without darts and tarts?"

. . .

That afternoon I walked around downtown Abu Dhabi looking
for the Ain Palace Hotel. I walked along the Corniche, with a
taste of cement dust on the tongue, along Hamdan Bin Mohammed Street, and past the Capital Garden. Here and there were
the pockets of small traditional streets I was looking for, wedged
between the skyscrapers and the malls, and here were fashion
shops with names like Swish and White Angel with completely
curtained display windows where nothing, therefore, was on
display. Alongside these were an inordinate number of laun-
dries and long walls with scraps of halfhearted graffiti: *I Love
Pakistan.*

The desert and nomad life feel close here, despite the thick ve-
neer of internationalism. The long, obscure history of an economy based on pearling, horses, falconry, ships, and then finally
oil. These were the Trucial States ruled by Britain until 1971.
First paved road: 1961. National dress: the *dishdasha.* The state
was opened to oil exploration in 1966 by its then ruler, Zayed bin
Al Nahyan Sultan. Since then it has become one of the richest,
and healthiest, nations on earth. It is legal for non-Muslims to
drink, but not in the street. Liquor can be purchased only in special government outlets, use of which requires a permit issued
by the Ministry of the Interior. There is a quiet asceticism here,
but not the tranquillity of an old Islamic city. The lines of the
streets have been destroyed to accommodate all those Western
towers; glass and steel soothe nobody. The asceticism is moral,
not material, and it is the puritanism of the desert peoples who

seem to have wandered into a world where other people's tastes have to be accommodated for the higher purpose of making money. Therefore there are bars.

The Ain Palace Hotel lies right behind the Corniche Cricket Club and the Sheikh Khalifa Energy Complex. It's an older hotel, once luxurious but now decidedly dejected, cramped and claustrophobic and filled with traveling Indian men attracted by its insalubrious reputation—insalubrious, that is, for those who have no need to go there in the first place. The hotel bar lies to one side of the lobby, safely invisible behind heavy doors, and the lobby after seven at night is shaped by the flow of these men and the occasional Chinese freelancers who make their way in and out of what exiles call the Ally Pally. But at eight that night, for some reason, there was almost no one there. The black-and-white floral wallpaper and glass wall lamps seemed to contain myself and three Chinese girls playing mah-jongg in a corner. Where were the lads? The barman said something about horse races that night. The girls looked bitter and very Harbin, but one of them came up anyway to try her luck. An ancient Western guy sat at the bar, listing sideways, a cigarette burning in the blue Foster's ashtray.

It's a British pub. Empires always leave behind places like this. It was a bar of global brands, of Smirnoff, Jim Beam, Magners Irish cider, Cutty Sark and Pernod, and then of generic premium gin and standard cognac served in multiples of 30ls for twenty to twenty-five dirhams a shot. In places like the Trucial States, it would have been the officers' mess that was the model for such pubs. A male space by definition and not ashamed of the fact. A half-pint of beer was about twelve dirhams. You could come here and drink Steinlager Edge and Breezer and Gaymers beer. The vast corporate alcohol industry that networks across the world was showcased in a single bar, offering to the Englishman a taste of home (or Singapore) and to the local who might happen to be here to drink a soda, a vision of industrialized uncleanness and temptation. They might both watch the rugby on the plasma TV, and they might both like the gold-sprayed chandeliers. But the *scent* of distilled liquor and spilled beer that defines a bar of this kind cannot be avoided. A Muslim friend in Dhofar once told me that, for him at least, it was like the smell of roasting pig: appalling and beckoning, and irresistible on the level not of appetites or mental desire but on the level of dopamine and the hormonal mysteries. "And therefore more dangerous," he said with the utmost gravity, "than you can possibly imagine."

And sitting there in the Ally Pally, I was suddenly overcome with nostalgia. England, my England: did you make me an inconsiderate drinker?

England, Your England

As A. A. Gill has said, "First drinks are important to alcoholics." It was in the mid-1970s that I used to take the train from Haywards Heath to Victoria Station while playing truant from school for the afternoon. I made my way to Soho where there was a pub called the Nellie Dean, a place that is still there, of course, the Nellie Dean of Dean Street. My first drink might have been there, but one is never sure, because I have talked about the Nellie Dean so many times with my father, who used to be a regular there, and now I cannot remember if my first drink was at the Nellie Dean or in the Witch on Sunte Avenue in Lindfield, a rural pub near our house that today serves, with a special kind of sadness, pad thai and grapefruit sorbet, or whether it was another place up on Berners Street. But I am pretty sure it was the Nellie Dean. Today I walk past it briskly, amazed at the amount of hanging greenery that stifles its facade and the golden glow from inside. It looks like a jeweler's box on some miserable nights.

The Nellie Dean was not just any pub, because it had once been called the Highlander and had only recently changed its name. I could go in when I was fifteen and no one threw me out. I started with shandy and worked up to shots of vodka. By now I had discovered a book called *Memoirs of the Forties* by the dandy, screenwriter, and sometime Duke of Redonda, Julian Maclaren-Ross. It was a book that I could not stop reading because it portrayed a part of London just south of Oxford Street, Fitzrovia, as a topology defined by pubs like the Wheatsheaf and the Highlander, between which this amazing man in his dark mirrored glasses, teddy bear overcoat, and gold-tipped cane rushed in search of daily audiences and small doses of satisfactory oblivion. Later he became the model for the down-at-heel writer Trapnel in Anthony Powell's *A Dance to the Music of Time*, but many have observed that Maclaren-Ross was anything but down-at-heel. He was half or quarter Indian, with a mixture of Scots and Latin American, and he seemed to me— dimly glimpsed through a book that came out in 1965—like a model of paranoid elegance befitting a character whose main energy was the creation of itself. He was, of course, a drinker of moving proportions, and it was because of Maclaren-Ross that I had been impelled to seek out the Highlander, which is now called the Nellie Dean.

Maclaren-Ross possessed several identities, between which he moved as the need arose. One was "Mr. Hyde." He invented himself as a multitude of personalities. Later in life he fell into poverty and could never finish the books he had long planned. Anthony Cronin describes him as a wandering drinker who perhaps squandered his considerable gifts on the spontaneous art form of the one-man monologue, fueled by alcohol: "He liked the myth of apparent failure; forms of revenge intrigued him and forms of mysterious return; the ruined gambler with one last throw, the heir who would reappear one stormy night, the Jacobite exile who would live to see the usurpers humbled." This was the legend of the drinker as a man who has inverted the normal rules of personality and the success that proceeds from them. The drink gave him curious characteristics. Verbal brilliance, ephemerality, nostalgia. It may have made him into a performer who could have immortalized himself more successfully through YouTube but who died too early, from a heart attack in 1964.

My father used to go to the Highlander because he worked nearby on Frith Street, and occasionally he would mention it when my mother was not around. In later years he claimed to have seen an extraordinary graffiti on the walls of the gents' in the Nellie Dean, which read, more or less as follows:

The Highlander with its pathetic documentarian pretensions is dead, thank Christ.

I was always aware that my mother drank more than my father, and that many imputed this flaw to her Irish origins. It is, for the English, a common accusation and revelatory of a cast of mind that does not care to submit a mirror-ward glance at its own epic alcoholic lawlessness. But my father, at least, was never a drinker in that sense. He liked his pint rather than his dram. His nickname for my mother was "Coffee," presumably in honor of her love of that drink, but the irony did not take long to adhere, and with time the sobriquet withered.

I felt, perhaps wrongly, that as they grew older, alcohol destabilized the intricate microcosm they had built around not just each other but around their three children as well. I and my two sisters were not even aware of this much of the time. It was a noble, defiant kind of denial, a self-submission to a higher interest—the family and the welfare of children—that was very English. And the way that drink made it both bearable and completely unstable was also very English. I was not sure, either at the time or since, whether to loathe it or feel grateful to it. The English relationship to drink is so deeply burned into my way of being in the world that to write about drink is to simultaneously write about England, a country I now know almost nothing about since I have lived in New York close to twenty years.

If you grew up in a steadfast English suburb of those years, you grew up steeped in booze. My parents kept a large drinks cabinet in their front room in Haywards Heath, with a folding minibar and mixers. It was fashionable at that time, long before wine was mainstream, to mix drinks in the early evening and serve them standing by the fire—gin and tonics with curls of shaved cucumber and Bloody Marys. When my father came back from his commute to a market research company in London, my mother would on occasion mix him a drink before dinner, and I noticed how it relaxed the atmosphere between them, unless my mother had gotten there first with a glass of

Famous Grouse, her favorite Scotch. Writing by herself at home, it was possible. A journalist and a talented radio playwright, she drank her Famous Grouse I imagine for inspiration, a habit that she has passed on, without inflicting upon me a taste for that lamentable Scotch.

Alcohol hovered in the air as an independent presence. It was always there, esoteric to the children but concrete in its familiarity. What would it have been like if my parents—or any parents of that time—had cheerfully smoked pot together every night after work? Many did in the late 1960s.

My parents, however, had decided to leave London partly in order to save their three children from the urban drug culture. They moved out in 1967, which was just in time, and bought a bank manager's house in the garden commuter town of Haywards Heath, where Harold Macmillan had retired.

Thus removed from the drug culture that would prospectively ruin them, their children were thrown into the suburban alcohol culture that would certainly affect them instead. Why alcohol rather than marijuana? The reasons were social: Haywards Heath was conservative and Little England. Only an hour from London and a half hour from Brighton and its "dirty weekends at the Metropole" extolled by T. S. Eliot, it was a fortress of private rectitude defended by a thousand lawns and yew hedges and scrolled gates. Behind these tall hedges stood the Victorian brick villas and the timbered Mock Tudors and the mansions with their service bells and dumbwaiters where isolated men and women could sink into their evenings with a glass of sherry and intoxicate themselves out of a present moment that offered little outside the home but long, dusky lanes and streets of closed shops and parks where the perverts gathered with their own bottles. It was a fine place to grow up.

Such a place was bound to encourage the use of a drug that was commensurately traditional. In the late 1960s, in Haywards Heath, pot was mentioned as a taboo. It seemed to come from far away, from the tropics, from America, from another dimension of life. Intoxication as an idea, however, was familiar. I remember someone at school telling me that Malcolm X used to get high on nutmeg. I looked it up. Nine megs of nutmeg was lethal, apparently, and there was nothing in the references about it making you high. I tried eight megs, an entire container, and mixed it with yogurt. It failed to make me high, but I threw up all night. Malcolm X must have had an extra additive up his sleeve. I was sure even after that that nutmeg could get me stoned, and I tried it several times afterward with no result. It seemed like an *easily disguised* habit to have.

Attached so firmly to the colonial past, filled with its retired soldiers and government officials, as well as aging spinsters and widows and young families seeking a safer, more English way of life, Haywards Heath was more suited to the drugs that had been used for centuries: the sherry, the beer, the Scotch.

The men went off in the morning to catch the 7:50 express train to Victoria, and the women stayed behind in their big empty houses listening to Radio 4 and bossing around the butcher deliverymen. Their lives were isolated, and then there were those tall yew hedges and lawns. You could never see the neighbors unless you bumped into them by accident walking down Summerfield Lane. Then they would stop for a moment, ask how the cats were, and move on.

So with my mother. On days when I was sick and staying at home, I remember the sound of her typewriter echoing through the house, and the radio turned up loud, and it was as if her past life were being guarded from submersion in her current life. I was sure that she had begun to drink.

She was a woman who had wandered almost by accident into a life she had not quite intended for herself. But as is often the case, a loyal and hardworking husband, a man with a sense of humor and an ability to love his children, had proved seductive. And why should it not be seductive? The drinker's legendary unhappiness and frustration are often exaggerated, and it is in any case an unhappiness that is much more complex than is suggested by the tinny word *circumstances*. A drinker is entangled in herself, unable to unravel the threads that have closed in upon her. The daily intoxication arises from an entire life's experience, not from an "illness" that is supposed to be less mysterious.

My mother dropped out of Durham University in her first year in 1953 and took a long experimental train journey across Europe to Naples. She was robbed on the train north of Rome and arrived in the Eternal City with nothing; an Irish priest, a friend of her family, took her in. The Tyneside Irish, of whom my mother was a member, were in those days severe Catholics (with a taste for spirited drinking), and the faith saved her in her hour of need. Rome in the middle of the Dolce Vita, fresh from the visits of Gregory Peck and Audrey Hepburn, must have been a youth in and of itself. But eventually, tiring of its tourism, she moved south to Naples, where she lived in Parthenope on the waterfront, teaching English to businessmen and making casual friends out of neighbors like Lucky Luciano and the best-selling Catholic novelist Morris West.

She later said that she could not have suffered to go back to Naples, to see its slow decline. But a decline from what? The city she knew was feral, the dark metropolis of Norman Lewis's brilliant book *Naples '44*. It must have been the first city in which she had been free, far from priests and family. The first place in which she had been able to be a woman.

There was a fearless insolence about her, a quality I saw years later on her deathbed. The suburban life of Haywards Heath after Naples, marriage after the life of a reporter on the lam, must have been a shock. As the years passed, she began to drink. My sister told me one day that she had noticed the family piano sounding a little strange when she played. Opening the lid, she found a bottle of vodka hidden under the strings. This was a secret between us, and we didn't talk about it for years. My own taste for drink, meanwhile, might be genetic, and it might have something to do with the Irish. Around us in those years in Haywards Heath hovered the shadowy outer family of the Tyneside Irish clan, the Grieves, the O'Kanes, and the O'Malleys, the male boozers who occasionally appeared at Christmastime and then disappeared like circus tricks, a nightmare fringe of shadow-puppet men with bright blue eyes and wet lips.

My uncle Michael, who died in a halfway home for alcoholics in Scotland, his foot recently amputated from diabetes, a man who had disappeared for a quarter century, abandoning his wife and children, to whom he had become a mysterious stranger. My great-uncle John O'Kane, publisher of the Liverpool University Press, who appeared every Christmas Eve with a different girl fresh off ocean liners and airplanes from Madrid, who would walk in the front door covered with snow and sit at the piano, pull up his cuffs, and begin to play and sing, uninvited, mad and drunk. A man who was convinced that he was admired and loved, and maybe even feared, but who was none of those. As a child, I adored him. He wore tweed suits and Italian ties and brought me jazz LPs from stores in Paris and Barcelona; his hands shook all the time, and he had those bloody oyster eyes that did not preclude tenderness. I remember, as he lay next to me in bed listening to "Purple Haze" (not the Jimi Hendrix song), his smell of booze and cologne mixed up, the inadvertent vibration of his body.

Here was a male gorgon who stormed around the world on "business" liquoring himself at a thousand bars, "that drunken Irish loafer," as my father called him, who didn't care about gathering moss as he rolled like a stone through his ramshackle life. I admired his fearlessness. I admired the way at Christmas dinner he toasted everyone singly and did it with neat Glenfiddich, and then burst—still uninvited—into one of his own inane compositions. What sound track must have been playing inside his formidable and erudite mind? The alcoholic wants to be loved, and just as fervently he wants to be hated and reviled.

Dreaded but unavoidable, the drunk is always at the bar of

life, like the man in Tati's *Playtime* who, despite being ejected from the lounge by the seat of his pants, always manages to reappear at the same spot. He is always there, irrepressible and stoic, doomed and melodic, while the teetotaler is home in bed, snoring next to a glass of water.

The moods of alcohol are like dabs of color on a psychotic palette that can be mixed at random. There are moments when intoxication induces a feeling of immersion in a vast and shadowy element. Walt Whitman ventures down to the shoreline and dissipates like "a little wash'd-up drift" into the ocean:

> Aware now that amid all that blab whose echoes recoil
>   upon me I have not once had the least idea who or
>   what I am,
> But that before all my arrogant poems the real Me
>   stands yet untouch'd, untold, altogether unreach'd,

We know this feeling. Crudely but also subtly, the bottle facilitates this solitude, and the drinker knows it all too well. He is canny about his possibilities. A self-critic, a connoisseur of his own altered states, he knows exactly how to tweak himself upward and downward. He is an amateur alchemist when it comes to the drinks themselves. If he were a writer and wanted to explain himself to strangers, he would write a book called *In Praise of Intoxication.* No one would invite him to explain his views in public. In America, he would not be taken seriously for a moment. But he would not be taken seriously by himself either: being taken seriously is not necessary to anything truly serious. The drinker is a Dionysiac, a dancer who sits still, a mocker. He doesn't need your seriousness or your regard. He just needs a little quiet music, and a gentle freedom from priests.

The Pure Light of High Summer

It was the Greeks who defined the subconscious Dionysian aspirations of the modern drinker, who could be imagined as a pagan remnant who has survived the purges of Christianity. Islam, ironically, gave us distillation just as the Greeks gave us fermentation. Distillation and fermentation: they could not be more different. One rational and scientific in origin, the other mystical and organic.

Dionysus is the god of vegetation, of the theater, of bulls, of women, and of wine. He is the destroyer and the liberator, "the god who crushes men." But he is the god who also demands that embryos not be harmed. His cult was dominated by women. Its practitioners were primarily female with a reputation for being "raving women," *mainas*. He was the god of what the Greeks called *zoe*, or indestructible collective life, as opposed to mere *bios*, the life of an individual. He emerged from the thigh of Zeus and was also known as *Dios phos*, "light of Zeus."

The Greeks themselves found him baffling and unnerving,

They struggled to find the words to describe him. Was he anthropomorphic, or was he like some element of the universe that could only be sensed indirectly? The poet Pindar, invoking his miraculous relationship to the blossoming of orchards, compared him with *hagnon phengos oporas:* "the pure light of high summer."

The great Hungarian scholar of Dionysus, Carl Kerényi, began his opus *Dionysos, Archetypal Image of Indestructible Life,* with a remarkable scholarly reverie on the subject of fermentation in Crete. Dionysus, he claimed, arose in some complex and obscure way from the fermentation symbolism of early Crete, where fermented honey and then beer suggested life emerging mysteriously from decay. It was fermentation itself that made Cretans think of the indestructibility of *zoe.* As things decay, they give off an enigmatic life; they bubble and seethe and self-transform. Like honey and mead, wine suggested *zoe* and seemed to partake in cosmic life. "A natural phenomenon inspired a myth of *zoe . . .* a statement about life which shows its indestructibility."

The rising of the star Sirius in July became, as with the Egyptians, the time of ritual fermenting—that is, the height of summer. Fermentation and intoxication must have seemed a mystical unity to the Cretans, who also consumed opium, according to Kerényi. The intoxication must have had religious import to them, and from honey and beer they transposed the symbolism to the richer, more luxurious wine. They called their sacrificial bulls "wine-colored" for no particular reason, and a thousand years later Greeks still carried bulls to the altar during Dionysian rites. Around this god many odd symbols crystallized for reasons we cannot now excavate. The bull, the snake, fermented grape juice, and the dolphins one sees on black-figured cups surrounding the ship where Dionysus sails alone under a mast of grapevines. They are the sailors who intended to kidnap him but were foiled and turned, by an act of godly mercy, into cetaceans.

The Cretans created a core mythology around this god of fermentation that the Greeks later continued, sometimes unknowingly. Though since Linear A, the actual language of the Cretans, has never been deciphered, we do not really know. The Minoan hieroglyph for *wine*, meanwhile, an ideogram in Linear B (early Greek translated into Cretan writing), is very like the Egyptian hieroglyph for the same thing, and we know from paintings of the Eighteenth Dynasty that Egypt already had a vast wine culture by the time Crete became rich, a viticulture that perhaps spread to Crete, as we can see from the Minoan *villa rustica* excavated at Kato Zakros. The vine was not Cretan or Greek, but in Europe its fermented fruit did become a singular god. A dense and complex core of symbols and myth passed into the occidental bloodstream, making wine a source of religious experience. It eventually became Christ's blood.

To this day the only place in Greece that is named after the god of wine is the Athens suburb of Sto Dionyso, a few miles north of Kifisia. (The others have been Christianized into "Saint

Dionysus.") In ancient times it was known as Ikarion. This mountain village might have been one of the first places that the new cult established itself around 1500 B.C., coming up from the coast of Attica. The ports of Attica, such as Porto Raphti and Thorikos, had Dionysian festivals in classical times and some of the oldest theaters, and perhaps they were where the first wine deity arrived by sea. It might have been from the Aegean island of Ikaria.

The god arrived. He went to the house of a man called Ikarion, who had a daughter named Erigone. Ikarion had little idea that the tall stranger was the son of Zeus and Semele or that he had been married to Ariadne. The stranger had a gift: a domesticated vine. The people of the Attic mountains only knew the wild vine. Ikarion planted the domesticated variety and under the stranger's instruction learned to make wine from it. He then poured his first vintage into pigskins and took them into the neighboring villages as a gift. Perhaps it was the god's instruction.

Not knowing what this new drink was, the villagers quaffed it like water and became murderously drunk. Thinking that Ikarion had poisoned them, they formed a mob and swept down on his house, where they killed him on the spot and buried him under a wild vine tree. When Erigone returned home, her dog, Maira, dug up the corpse.

Erigone then hanged herself in grief from this same tree, from which bunches of wild grapes hung. Father, daughter, and dog were compassionately turned into constellations by the gods (Ikarion became Boötes, Erigone became Virgo, and the dog was converted into Canis Minor). Later, in classical times, Erigone was remembered by the young girls of Athens in a curious festival called the Aiora, or "the feast of the swinging chairs," during which they swung themselves from trees in little chairs to imitate the giddy sensation of being drunk. This took place the day before the Dionysian Festival and reminded its celebrants, one assumes, that Dionysus was a god of death and sacrifice as well as a god of stage plays and blossoming orchards and wine. In other versions of the myth, Erigone was actually the god's wife, and in yet others it was Dionysus himself who was torn to pieces and then miraculously reconstituted.

The tame vine—the *hemeris*—arrives in Attica as a mysterious gift, and it is the god who makes that gift. The gift by its very nature has to be shared, consumed, and is at the beginning devoid of commercial instrumentality. Wine, in fact, is often portrayed as a "gift," an enjoyment and a balm that has no functional use to the human body and is not at all a food. The god donates it, and it circulates freely, entering into everyone's bloodstream until it becomes a kind of binding agent that holds a mass of individuals together. It is shared, and it is sacral.

Lewis Hyde discusses Kerényi's book on Dionysus in his great work *The Gift*. He remarks that in later times the Greek worshippers of Dionysus "would sing of the dismemberment of their god as they crushed the grapes through the winepress. Dionysos is a god who is broken into a higher life. He returns from his dismemberment as strong or stronger than before, the wine being the essence of the grapes and more powerful."

Hyde says this about drink itself: "Moreover, when the fermented liquid is drunk, the spirit comes to life in a new body. Drinking the mead is the sacrament of reconstituting the god."

The vineyard workers of the Mediterranean were ordered by imperial decree in 691 to stop crying "Dionysos!" at harvest time and to cry instead "Kyrie Eleison!" It was the sixth year of the reign of Emperor Justinian II. The Byzantine Empire was in crisis as the Arabs launched assault after assault against it. The effect of this Islamic war against the Byzantines is hard to fully gauge. It is possible that the iconoclastic crisis a century later—when icons and images were banned throughout the empire—was a response to Islam's seemingly successful severity. In 692 Justinian convened a council known as the Quinisextum that issued 102 canons. It was a watershed, a final denial of classical and pagan culture.

In the 102 canons many things were banned. The pagan festival of Brumelia, where the citizens of Constantinople dressed in disguises and danced through the streets, was abolished. Mimes, pantomimes, and spectacles with wild animals were suppressed. Canon 24 prohibited priests from attending the theater or watching games in the Hippodrome. Canon 62 outlawed women dancing in the streets and the wearing of female dress by men. Invoking the name of Dionysus passed into history. Young men were also forbidden from leaping over bonfires to celebrate the summer solstice.

Dionysus, then, was banished as part of a widespread suppression of public pleasure and pagan freedoms. It was a vast piece of social engineering intended to Christianize the empire once and for all and to make it more like its bitter rival, Islam. (It did nothing to save Justinian, who was soon deposed and defaced by having his nose cut off, so that he was henceforth known as Rhinometos, the "noseless." He later returned to the throne, presiding over an empire forever altered by his legislation.)

A Christian, however, still drinks wine as a symbol of the blood of a Christ who has been sacrificed, scattered, and reconstituted. Dionysus, a glamorous and youthful male god who incarnates the fermenting mysteries of *zoe*, or eternal life, is highly suggestive. He is the god who transforms and intoxicates women, whose element is an alcoholic drink.

Greek religion suggested a "Dionysus-dominated universalism." Dionysus, in other words, spread all over the Roman world and became a world religion. In the tombs of the dead, images of Dionysus were especially common, as Kerényi writes, "for it was in connection with the burial of the dead that the need to celebrate indestructible life was most absolute and universal. This is as true of the Dionysian religion as it is of Christianity. The amplification of the Dionysus cult in late antiquity to a cosmic, cosmopolitan religion was a very natural development, but such a development was possible only insofar as *zoe* could exert a spontaneous religious influence. This influence, in the mythological and cultic forms here described, had a historical limit."

But it survives. The drinker slouching his way every night toward his bar-shaped Bethlehem is searching for his or her own version of Pindar's amazing intuition. We want, even for a few moments, the "pure light of high summer" inside us. For Pindar was suggesting not that Dionysus was like that light, but that he *was that light.* The god as summer's light itself: intoxication as pure immanence.

New Year's in Muscat

The worst time of year for the drinker is Christmas and New Year's. It may be the worst time for everyone, but for the determined and solitary drinker it has a coercive and dismal quality, because suddenly your private vice becomes a public virtue in which you are obliged to participate as if nothing has changed. Drinking not only increases and becomes more social; it becomes part of the actual rite of this long-devastated Christian holiday, which would be better renamed the Winter Solstice with Shopping and Antidepressants. Post-Christians by the millions flee to Bangkok, Dubai, and the Seychelles to escape the misery of their ancestral rites. They cannot bear the thought of family rooms with twinkling fir trees and TV marathons endured with the aid of sherry. They want sun, blue skies, nightlife, and no trace of Santa.

Inconveniently, places like Bangkok and Dubai try their best to make the holiday crowds feel at home by thrusting Santas and Christmas trees at them at every turn. In Bangkok there are even choirs of schoolgirls in little Santa outfits ringing bells in the department stores. It's good business to make *farangs* feel homesick.

In the lobby of the Four Points Sheraton on Sheikh Zhayed Road in Dubai, where my Italian lover and I had just arrived on Christmas Day (there is no better Christmas Day than one spent thirty thousand feet up in the air with a gin and tonic), there was a tall Christmas tree shimmering with baubles and miniature tin sleighs. Islam had not precluded this racket, and there were even yuletide jingles in the elevator. The Italian, Elena, in all her blond and oddly Nordic magnificence, grimaced and said straightaway that her first time in the Gulf had already been a little spoiled by all this European *tack*. The decision not to spend the holiday with either of our families should at least have been rewarded with total cultural displacement. No such luck. "I could listen to this in Milan." She scowled, and put her hands over her ears. At least, I said, we could drink.

We were planning to drive from Dubai to Muscat in Oman, where we would spend New Year's. Oman was the only country in the region I had not been to, and I was curious to see how a New Year's could be spent in that small jewel-city whose name reverberated in the English mind. Muscat. What would midnight at New Year's be like in Muscat, as far away as either of us could get from the usual tumult of that occasion?

It was true that we could drink in Dubai at least. Not on the street, and not everywhere, but certainly on the rooftop bar of the Four Points. From there we could see the whole city-state and the edges of the burned desert just beyond. I used to come there frequently once upon a time, and I had an assortment of memories about Dubai.

I wrote articles about Emaar, the ruling family's construction company that had built the Palms, the grotesque developments that stretched out to sea in the shape of those emblematic trees. Sometimes I flew into Dubai just to dry out at the Al Rolla suites on the street of that name in Bur. Whole weeks just lying in bed and drinking mineral water and eating Persian food and sitting at the edge of a tiny pool waiting for my head to clear. I noticed that Western observers never ceased raising their fingers at the moral turpitudes of Dubai. It was autocratic, a slave state, millions of indentured Indian and Filipino servants. If you passed wind, they assured us, you would be arrested and thrown into jail by the religious police. The place had no identity. It was "artificial," it was "soulless," it was amoral and immoral and hypocritical.

Johann Hari, the most indignant of journalists given over to permanent indignations, wrote an exposé on the place in which he met a woman living in a car. Yes, a woman living in a car! A European woman who couldn't pay her bills! It's a common form of moral gossip. This, from people happily living their lives in the United States and Europe. That Dubai is a mirror image of ourselves created to please us and flatter us had occurred to some of them. But how did you digest this extraordinary fact?

What bothered them most about Dubai was that it was an Arab country that had an infrastructure and a per capita income superior to their own. It was Arab, but it worked, as least materially. No one flying out of an inept airport like Heathrow or JFK and arriving at Dubai International could fail to be disturbed in some way. Which facility more suggested decay and decline?

Arab societies must be failures across the board, and if one of them is not, other condemnations must be found. I used to wonder if New York, where I live, really had any more "identity" than Dubai just because its public transport was an underfunded sewer or its roads could not be paved beyond the levels found in the poorer suburbs of Kingston. Fifty billion dollars a year in city budgets and barely surfaced roads. Did Manhattan these days, that Disneyland diorama, have a surfeit of "identity" that Dubai lacked? Did Paris or central London, those tourist facilities pretending to be cities? Dubai was what it was, a place on the make, a place coming from nowhere. That is, from the desert. Its population was Indian and Tamil and Pakistani and Lebanese and Chinese, its whores were from Harbin and Ulan Bator, and its wastrels spoke the Arabic of Beirut and Cairo, the Farsi of exiles, and the variegated English of the internationally uprooted.

I never found this cocktail entirely tedious, which is all one can ask of a city these days. Where Brooklyn and Hoxton and the Eleventh Arrondissement seemed afflicted by a dated preciousness, not to mention a growing lack of identity, I found Dubai grimly interesting. Brash, unnerving, and false, but not dull, not starved of identity, as if identity were a nutrient that never failed to deliver.

The concession to alcohol is the most surprising facet of this minuscule kingdom. It has been made for financial reasons, but it is a concession all the same. The Emirates are religiously conservative. (There's "identity" for you; it's just not an identity we like.) The decision of the Maktoubs, the ruling dynasty, to permit alcohol widely throughout their own emirate was a bold one. It made the city more Western, more tolerant, more indistinguishable from occidental cities, as it was intended to do. It was this quality that led to the charge of soullessness and a dearth of identity. The managers of Emaar used to say, more or less, "Damned if you do, damned if you don't."

Elena and I went drinking every night. I took her one night to the notorious bar of the York Hotel, a pickup scene, and we drank whisky sours among a crowd of Chinese girls who were more toasted than we were. Indian businessmen swarmed through that small lobby area looking like wide-awake sleepwalkers. Sex and booze are always in each other's company, handmaidens to each other. The York is a wild bar. We also went to the Lebanese places where you can drink a bottle of Jumblatt's Kefraya or a Le Brun arak, and you can drink them deep into the night. There was the pleasure of being with this beautiful, headstrong, unfaithful girl and drinking with her inside our emotional cocoon. Elena seemed, in fact, quite anxious about the prospect of *not* being able to drink in Oman.

"They can drink in that country, can't they?" she kept asking. "It's New Year's. There's only one thing I insist on at New Year's, and that's a bottle of champagne. Is champagne legal in Oman?"

"Of course it is. Would I be taking you to a place for New Year's where champagne was illegal?"

"I never know with you, *bestia*. You're such a lush, you don't even think about things like that."

"I thought about it. Champagne is legal in Oman."

In reality, I had no idea if it was or not. I knew nothing about Oman.

"But *The Lonely Planet*," she objected, "says it's more conservative than Dubai. Much more. What if champagne is illegal?"

"Then we'll have a dry New Year's."

"A dry New Year's? There's no way I am having a *dry* New Year's. What is a dry New Year's? It's nothing. New Year's without champagne is nothing."

"Agreed," I said.

When we drank together, the moods came thicker and faster, and they were different moods. The tensions, normally latent and indistinguishable from inertia, sparkled at the surface and acquired a menacing eloquence.

"I don't want an Islamic New Year," she whispered. "I mean, I respect the culture and everything, but not on New Year's. And I don't want any lectures from you about not being local and all that bullshit. I want a bottle of *cold* champagne."

"You will have it, *polpetta principessa*."

The relationship driven, or watered, by drink has its own rules and its own rhythms, even when we are not aware of them. The suppression of alcohol is itself a sexual suppression. Alcohol is the fuel of desire, and to prohibit it is to prohibit the flow of male and female and, if you like, to prohibit the movements of erotic pursuit.

I used to think with Elena that there were moments that could not have existed without alcohol. Not just the explosive rows and

recriminations, the scenes of rage, but the lovemaking, which
left bruises and scars (treasured and left as were), and the moments of falling off into a sleep that was deeper. Alcohol shared
has a different effect. I wondered, in fact, if our relationship was
disintegrating as my parents' had done, under the influence of
a drug, because it cannot be denied that one says very different things when under that influence, just as one fails to *not*
say things. The equilibrium of tact and sensitivity, of careful,
ongoing thoughtfulness, breaks down in a storm of unframed
emotion. The words slip and keel over, and things of incredible brutality and unnecessary truthfulness are said. And yet
I also watched her head on the pillow, angelic and icily blond,
the hair disordered, the hands seized up as if in the middle of
an incomplete gesture—the sleep of the drinker. But not that of
the alcoholic or the abuser of drink. The sleep of the woman in
whom the Dionysian thread has not been broken by prohibition
and misuse and the misogyny of the Teetotaler God.

It is easy to leave Dubai by car, and swift. A few miles on the
road toward Hatta, and the glitz is left behind. Thorn trees,
a gray gritty desert of drinn and wavelike sand, and the wild
camels nosing their way along the *oueds*. Many visitors take to
dune-buggying and two-night desert camps, which are invariably luxurious, but few drive into Oman from the Emirates. At
the edge of the Al Hajar Mountains, the Omani border post just
beyond Hatta in the hills is housed in a vast and palatial building well stocked in images of the country's ruler, Sultan Qaboos,

a man who dethroned his father in 1970 and then survived a violent Marxist rebellion—the Dhofar Rebellion—with the timely aid of the British SAS and the incomparable David Smiley.

Qaboos has been mildly favorable to the British ever since. Nowhere else in the Middle East, or indeed the world, can you sit at an outdoor café in a city square and watch huge screens relaying the Changing of the Horse Guard—an equestrian spectacle much appreciated by the audience. His country has also become rich through oil, making his quaint monarchy stable in the trickle-down way. Despite unrest during the Arab Revolution, the country's low unemployment, magnificent infrastructure, and relative absence of ghetto poverty have held it firm for the moment. It has been agitation spilling over from Yemen that has most concerned the elderly, benign Qaboos. Al Qaeda are here on the desert roads.

It is a country of sea and desert constantly meeting, of small towns and oases, with no large city other than Muscat, which is not a large city. On the radio, the religious sermons begin as soon as you cross the border and descend through iron-dark mountains toward the beach-town lights of Suhar on the Indian Ocean.

The coast road then plunges south three hundred miles to the capital. A wide, six-lane marvel, fast, with no police. At the edge of the land cling white villages set against an indigo sea. Indian immigrants swarmed the intersections, running across the freeway to get to the lines of neon-lit restaurants on the other side. You catch their laughter in passing. Risk of death for a nice curry. On the landward side stand freshly painted mosques and banks set in landscaped palm gardens, opulent petrol stations where you pay eight dollars to fill the tank. There is no public transport. Everyone has a car because they are so cheap to run. Not a bus in sight, just the speed and lights of oil-funded superhighways. And yet this American template has not produced an American result. Arab pop music on the airwaves, but little of the Western variety. In the villages and even the towns, the quiet domesticity, the closedness of the traditional Islamic settlement, prevails. No crime, no disturbance.

The old town of Muscat is a mixture of government offices and open-air museum with, at its center, Qaboos's Ali Baba royal palace. It is lightly guarded, and its windows face directly onto the ocean, onto piles of rocks where the waves crash. Muscat is a city of forts. Every hillside is crowned by walls, towers, and battlements. The hills themselves rise like jagged piles of pig iron, almost black. The sea is everywhere, yet it does not ruffle the miniaturized stolidity of the city.

One cannot stay there. The hotels for the foreigners, the all-in resorts, are clustered a little farther on around the village of Al Bustan and the remoter fishing village of Qantab, which itself is untouched, or else near the fashionable seaside neighborhood of Qurm on the other side of the city. In these two locales you will find the Intercontinentals and the Shangri-las, the Hyatts and the Radissons, oases of alcohol within a dry nation. They were all booked solid for the holidays. Oman is popular among the British middle classes with a taste for buffets and artificial beaches.

We drove to the Shangri-la near Qantab to inquire about a

room. A grandiose setting, among the desert cliffs and coves. But inside, a suffocating scallop of a hotel filled with people who would clearly not set foot outside for a week. Arabia here was present as a motif in the restaurant and lobby decor, the pendant iron lamps and the dining tents set out at night along the man-made beach. There was a bar, and it was stocked, and people were drinking at it, but this would not offset the wider misery of staying here. But they were, in any case, fully booked. We walked around Muscat in the late afternoon, in that landscape of military wariness and embattlement, walls within walls within keeps, and then drove back to the modernized suburb of Al Ghubrah, where we knew of a more commercial hotel called the Al Midan Suites, popular among business travelers. It sat among construction sites and next to a school. There was a Thai restaurant on the ground floor, but because it was next to the school, it was forbidden to sell alcohol. A dry hotel, but they had rooms.

We unpacked and lay on the bed. The sea could be seen just beyond the parking lots and cranes. A whole day without a drink, and I could already sense the slight anxiety that this had aroused. Elena crawled on top of me and said, "Drink or *amore?* Which one first?" *Amore,* then, but soon after the drink. We went down into a cool, breezy night and an empty street. There was nowhere to drink, and Al Ghubrah is a lively neighborhood without tourists. We drove to Qurm, a short voyage along the Qaboos Freeway, and parked by the sea promenade. A path wound along the low cliffs and along a wide beach lit with fires, and around it stood *shawarma* cafés and fruit juice bars. It was our first evening alone without alcohol, perhaps ever. Walking under stars, along that lonely path, I felt myself sinking slowly back to earth, a feather descending, and I was sure that this was true of us as a couple as well. Nevertheless, we continued to speculate on where we could get a drink. It became a game between us. Where could we get a drink without going into an overbearing hotel?

Slowly, hour by hour, the crisis of *not drinking* was developing. The crisis of being alone with each other without mediation, alone without stimulation or distortion or the slight drama of the drink, the sexual release of the drink.

Alcohol stimulates the receptors for the neurotransmitter dopamine. Dopamine, along with adrenaline and serotonin, is one of the oldest neurotransmitters in the brain and is shared with most mammals and even, it is thought, with fruit flies. It is associated with pleasure, locomotion, and motivation, and it also mediates addiction through its ability to reinforce pleasure.

This ancient, primitive chemical inside us keeps us alive in a very basic way; the dopamine neurons produced in the substantia nigra part of the brain are to some extent what makes us enjoy being alive. A rare disease called familial Mediterranean fever is said to destroy dopamine receptors in humans and produces a condition known as anhedonia: the inability to feel pleasure. Alcohol is also thought to have an adverse effect upon the neurotransmitter GABA, gamma-aminobutyric acid, which governs inhibition in the mammalian nervous system.

The purest stimulator of dopamine is cocaine, but alcohol is close behind, though it is in some respects "dirtier," more complex, and more dangerous because it hits more receptors than just dopamine. Yet because it can flush us with dopamine, it is also life giving, exultant, sense enhancing, and liberating. It wounds slowly as it awakens.

Perhaps this is why sobriety feels, at first, so solitary. There is no intensification of life, no rush, and inhibition—that is, separation—returns. Alcohol is able to create a feeling of togetherness when it is drunk in company, especially when it is drunk by a man and a woman together. The solitary alcoholic is only one aspect of drinking. There is also the couple bound together, united and freed by it, their bodies flooded with dopamine, their GABA repressed. This creates closeness and giddy ease, a losing of the mind that is not only desirable but necessary.

This loosening of the chemical structure of the nervous system is important in friendship, too, because it increases spontaneity and frankness, affection, and temporary selflessness. It is like walking away from the GABA-bound self for a while, and it is this that we identify as the conviviality of alcohol. But with the couple, it is even more important. The tensions of lovers are not easy to resolve day by day, night by night, and alcohol is one of the means whereby open moods are induced. Those moods can also create the macabre scenes of *Who's Afraid of Virginia Woolf?*

A relationship between a drinker and a teetotaler is a parlous one. The teetotaler feels misunderstood and is resentful of the drinker's facile elasticity and tendency to overstate, to forgive and enjoy the passing moment. The drinker resents the tee-totaler's rigidity, primness, and limited ability to let go of her relentless mental clarity. Her clarity—despite its beauties—is irritatingly pedestrian in the end. Each finds the other a bore.

The drinker knows that life is not mental and not a matter of control and demarcation. The teetotaler, on the other hand, knows full well how even a molecule of alcohol changes body and mind. The Muslim, the Protestant puritan, and the tee-totaler are kin; they understand the world in a very similar way, despite all their enormous differences, while the drinkers, too, understand the world in a way that unconsciously unites them. They know that the parameters that contain us are not all human, let alone divine. You could say even that dopamine unites us for a short spell with drunken fruit flies and happy dogs. It takes us out of the boring, two-dimensional misery of the human.

Since we were now dry, we began to get up early and drive through Muscat to the beach near Qantab, with nothing in mind other than hiring a fishing boat and exploring beaches farther down the coast. It was a landscape of dark ocher stone, headlands carved by wind, the coves behind them sealed off from the interior by desert scrub. Across that volatile sea went the aquamarine boats of the Omani fishermen always looking for a quick deal. At the end of these days, isolated on a cove with no one else, I would feel panic at being so soberly remote.

On some days we forwent the boats and drove down the coast

road toward Sur. The villages feel abandoned to the rhythms of the sea. Dibab, Fins, Bamah. The beaches at desert's edge, wind-swept and austere, paths running between flattened gardens of okra. We lay together in the wilderness, making words out of pebbles on the beach, walking through the dunes. We talked less and less, but this did not matter in the way that it might have mattered a few weeks earlier. I noticed that she was more withdrawn and that she was not unhappy to be withdrawn. But from what was she withdrawn?

The days at the desert sea were crystal clear, in terms of consciousness. It takes several days for all traces of alcohol to leave the bloodstream, and when that happens, the clarification is surprising. You move differently, you think differently; you sense things differently. You intuit your lover differently. There was something nightmarish about it. And at the same time it was a salvation. The eroticism changed shape.

If we had been drinking, we would have made love on the distant beaches, an act that would probably have led to our ar-rest. Without drink, we were more mindful, more aware of our responsibilities. A different kind of respect for each other emerged. But the trashy, slippery treachery underlying every-thing became more obvious.

Sometimes the fights were like something decaying in slow motion, a peach in a bowl caught in a weeklong film. They were caused by suspicions and manias that remained quiescent when we were sober but that alcohol brought into consciousness in an unstoppable way. A decay in which one could suddenly see the nasty end of things. I wondered then if I had suggested Oman simply because I knew it would be dry. Rancorous and violent evenings would be impossible in the Islamic monarchy by the sea, and we would be forced back into the level-headed banality that is sometimes what saves us from other people.

New Year's, however. That day we drove to the desert town of Nizwa and back. We arrived in Muscat tired and dusty and dressed up for the one night we had decided we would score a serious drink. The receptionists at the Al Midan took a dim view of trying to find a bottle of champagne anywhere outside a Western megahotel. We said we would go and have a look. In all of them it was three hundred dollars a head for New Year's dinner with a bottle of bad bubbly, usually Mumm, thrown in for the midnight hour. Exorbitant, then, but as eight o'clock approached and the year began to expire, it seemed irrelevant how much we would have to pay to sip the intoxicant. Four hundred, five hundred, we would have paid it. Elena's face began to harden as the dim possibility of not finding it at all began to occur to her. A determination appeared.

"We'll find somewhere," she said as we went out to the car. "A bottle of champagne at midnight is the *one* thing I insist on."

In Muscat you have to navigate through huge roundabout intersections, along lonely unmarked roads fringed with malls and developments, inside which your destination often lies. To get to Qurm, where the nearest hotels lay scattered along the beach, we had to get onto the Qaboos Freeway and find an exit that would take us to the Hyatt and the Radisson. By the time we got there, we saw below the drive a garden party under way with a crowd of people in paper hats. The New Year's party.

"No," Elena said, turning away, "I can't do it, baby. I can't sit at one of those tables and pretend I'm enjoying myself."

"You get a bottle of Mumm's."

"It's not even good champagne."

Do we care if it's good? I thought. *Is that what we are after, quality?*

We drove to the Radisson, which sits on top of a hill at the end of Qurm. It was a madhouse. The Persian restaurant had a few places still free, as it was also three hundred dollars a head with the bottle of champagne. The tables were packed with all the infidel refugees fleeing Islam's alcohol laws for the night. We took one look and wilted. "Come and join us," the manager kept crying, making sinister gestures at these overloaded tables. "It's your last chance in Muscat for a midnight drink! Everywhere is now booked, sir."

It was eleven, and we had one hour to find that elusive bottle, but we were not tempted to lay our quest to rest at the Persian restaurant of the Radisson. We went grimly back to the car. "One hour," she said. "We have one hour to not be fucked for New Year's."

The reportedly hedonistic seafront boulevards of Qurm, a string of cafés and restaurants where Muscat's beautiful people liked to parade themselves, yielded nothing but fruit juice. "They're drinking fruit juice on New Year's," Elena gasped. "I'm in hell." We came to a turnoff and took it, blindly hoping it would go back to the freeway. We stopped at one of the hotels and asked if they knew of any restaurants where we could get a drink at this late hour. The staff patiently looked up alternatives.

Yes, they said, there was a Mexican place in the neighborhood of Madinat Qaboos, in a mall. They drew us a map. They looked dubious. Good luck!

It was one of those small, friendly malls the Omanis seem to love, with restaurants and pleasure gardens tucked behind the retail outlets. We parked and walked down a lane into a series of restaurant gardens hung with lanterns where Omani crowds were smoking their *shish* and perhaps looking at their watches as carefully as we were. We hurried. There was a large Omani place called Kharjeen with gardens filled with trees, and behind it the Mexican joint. It had saloon swing doors and piñatas hung in the interior gloom. We went in frantically. It was filled with drunken tourists and expats in Stetsons and Omani guys on the prowl, and we knew at once that we couldn't do it. We retreated baffled into the alley, and there was a hysterical scene. It was ten to midnight, and we were to celebrate the hour dry. Our resolutions had come to nothing. There was little else to do but sit in the lovely gardens of Kharjeen and order *shuwa* marinated with pepper and turmeric with two tall watermelon juices. The moon rose over the garden, and the affluent Omanis did not look at their watches.

Elena had calmed a little, and when she had accepted the idea that we would not be drinking a bottle of champagne, she felt less hysterical, and we sipped the watermelon juices and waited. A great calm, suddenly. Midnight, and nothing happened. Everyone kept talking, eating, smoking, and no one even looked up. We kissed and wondered if we had miscalculated the time. The orgy of midnight never happened.

We toasted the New Year with fruit juice and then ordered apple *shish* pipes. The mania of the half-hour before midnight was forgotten, and we stayed in the garden for a long time, looking at the moon and smoking and saying very little. It was the first nonalcoholic New Year I had enjoyed since the age of thirteen. Here I was outside with the moon, smoking with the girl I adored, sober, clear, drinking *kharwa* coffee and not talking. The manic dialogues and monologues of alcohol absent. It was not bad. It was even preferable. We drove home very calmly, curiously contented, and amused ourselves half the night in our hotel bed, indifferent to the concept of a new year.

The following morning we got up early, hangover-free, and drove in the hard light to Qantab. The usual suspects were waiting for us, and we had a boat within minutes. The sea was calm and slightly menacing, as if hammerheads were waiting below.

We went to a new beach twenty minutes south. It was a narrow crescent of sand between two stone headlands that pushed out to sea like the prongs of a fork. The boatman left us in shallow water, and we waded ashore. He would be back at the end of the day. We climbed onto the sand, and within a minute we were alone. Behind us was a hillside of dry grasses and rubble, no road in sight. At the distant tops of the rock shelves, birds sat waiting.

We spread the towels and lay there in the gathering heat. I was glad now not to have a hangover. We had become saner as a result. However, looking up from my doze, I saw that Elena's eyes were wide awake, and that she was biting her lip nervously. She sat up then and began to look up and down the beach as if she had heard something unusual.

"I heard a bee," she said.

There are moments in every relationship when something is revealed that has never been seen before. I had never known that she had a fear of bees, or that bees occupied any place in her subconscious. Prolonged sobriety, perhaps, had begun to expose it.

"There's a bee here," she said then, getting up and standing there in the sunlight, magnificently Monica Vitti, tanned and blond and windblown, a girl who had been a dancer.

"There can't be a bee," I said.

"There's a bee. I can hear it." She began to sweat. "It's looking at me. I can feel it looking at me."

"I can't be looking at you."

"It's after me. Where is it?"

She began to wring her hands, then to pace back and forth. She began to cry. Then, suddenly she took off down the beach, screaming and waving her arms at an imaginary pursuing bee. She ran all the way down to the end of the little beach and began to dance about, battling phantom beasts. With a cry, she jumped into the water.

"I have cultivated my hysteria," Baudelaire once wrote, "with pleasure." I lay there not knowing what to do. I got up. At that moment a bee flew over my head and meandered its way down to the water's edge, but at the opposite end of the beach. Its indifference to us was obvious. I walked down the beach, wondering what I should say to comfort her. Now I wished we had a bottle of vodka to share. It would have made everything better. As I came up, she glared at me and demanded to know where the bee was. I lied that there was no bee.

"There's hammerhead sharks in there," I said.

She jumped out of the water back onto dry land and stood shivering, wildly looking around for signs of an attacker with little wings. I gave her the towel and told her to swat the air around her to keep the bees at bay. She seized the thing and did just that. We walked back to our place. Elena swatted the air around her, and soon she began to enjoy the swatting in itself. I lay down, and she paced up and down, swatting and then doing a few dance moves. It was a phobic trance.

Soon she was doing a full-blown number, leaping up and down, pirouetting on the sand, the towel flapping around her to keep off the bee. It became a performance, and the deep strangeness of the scene was offset by its sheer prettiness. At that moment an Arab fishing boat came into view slogging its way across the open water. It came halfway across the cove, and then it stopped, as if stupefied by what the crew had seen. A blond girl of obvious loveliness prancing about naked and capable of professional moves and waving a towel in one hand. I could see the hands raised to shade their eyes. Infidels, there was no end to their weirdness.

I thought about this all the way back to Dubai. We never had a drink in Oman, and the whole voyage had been alcohol-free from the first moment to the last. Its atmosphere had been unforgettable. There was something missing, some romantic

plumpness of mind was not there, and we had felt lean and sincere and too exposed. I had felt subtly accountable, like a charla-
tan who has been forced to take a lie detector test.

Back at the Four Points in Dubai, I went down alone to the
bar and ordered my usual vodka tonic. I was relieved to see the
eastern European tarts and to see the dartboard on the wall.
Elena was asleep upstairs, the incident of apiphobia long forgotten, and I was mentally free to rejoin the great brotherhood of
drinkers. I sank the vodka into my throat and sang a silent hal-
lelujah. Vodka: it is like an enema for the soul. The word means
"the little water," and I drank three Bong and tonics one after
the other, not thinking, not talking, just concentrating on my
reelevation into normalcy. And yet there was a thread of sadness
in this return, a nostalgia. That word in Greek simply means
"the pain of returning."

The Little Water

There used to be a game one could play in the cornfields of Haywards Heath with the lumbering combine harvesters that toiled there in summer. The drivers were unable to see anything on the ground, which invited a grim game that could be called a variation of African Chicken. We took turns swigging from a bottle of vodka stolen from our parents, drinking shots out of the metal cap. The Smirnoff tasted like fuel, like something scooped out of the bottom of an engine, but its little kick of heat at the end was addictive. We lay in the path of the combine harvesters, hidden in the wheat, then rolled away from the rotating blades at the very last minute. Lying there in the cool of the wheat stalks, totally out of your mind, you could hear the harvester approaching and could judge its distance aurally. Then, making a split-second decision, you rolled away as the blades whirled past.

Vodka made this possible. I looked up at the sky, and my mind dissipated into it, and I thought, *I'll be chopped to pieces, and I won't feel a thing. It'll be over in a second.*

I think it was I who stole the vodka bottles. When I drink a vodka tonic now in any bar in the world, I think for some reason of my parents in their airy house on Summerfield Lane opening bottles of Canada Dry and mixing it with Smirnoff and little wedges of lemon. It is perhaps a mistake of memory, but I see them there anyway. They look extraordinarily merry.

The Smirnoff labels with their fake czarist chic can trigger such memories. "The little water" became a fashionable drink sometime in the early 1970s, largely because of the brilliant advertising campaigns of Smirnoff. Vodka was cunningly introduced into the global diet, far more successfully than wine or other spirits. It brought different qualities to the glass: Nordic cleanliness and purity, a steely exotic chic ruthlessly exploited by the men who invented the Swedish government product known as Absolut in 1979.

The biggest drinks globally are Bacardi, Smirnoff, and Absolut. Ninety-six million liters of Absolut alone are drunk every year, and its ad campaigns are the longest running in history. Absolut is what you dependably find in a bar in the Middle East, and it is sold in 126 countries—a market saturation with few equals. It's an Absolut world, as their campaigns insist, and although the imams of Islam would disagree with this statement, the brand is ubiquitous wherever there is a bar.

I once was asked by *Vogue* to write a story about the two men who had invented Absolut, the entrepreneur Peter Ekelund and the master distiller Börje Karlsson. The two men had now invented another vodka, a vintaged potato vodka called Karlsson's Gold, which is made from six genetic strains of new potatoes in the Bjäre Peninsula on the west coast of Sweden. They have fetching names: the Celine, the Hamlet, the St. Thora, the Princess, the Solist, and the Marine. Most important is the Gammel Svensk Rod, or Swedish Red, which is one of the few potato species whose genetic patent is not owned by Monsanto. They are harvested by a cooperative of fanatical farmers who clean each one by hand.

Bjäre is where Ingmar Bergman shot his film *The Seventh Seal*. Remote and windswept, it is considered the Bordeaux of vodka potatoes. Ekelund met me at one of the farms and encouraged me to man one of the potato-harvesting machines that cross the fields like chugging tanks. We then went into one of the hangars and met the farmers to eat some raw potatoes. It seems they all have different aromas and textures. I was asked to introduce myself to the gathering, and for a joke I announced myself as "America's greatest vodka critic." I expected them to laugh and slap their knees, but no, with grinding Scandinavian seriousness, they nodded and looked a little apprehensive.

"So," one of them said, "you are the vodka critic for *Vogue*?"

Vodka for them was everything, and the idea of *Vogue* having a vodka critic seemed perfectly normal. I was bound to admit that I was. After which I was condemned to drink every sample of distillate on offer and make criticisms of them.

Karlsson's vodkas have a scent of white chocolate, and they are the ones I always want in my vodka martini, though Professor Karlsson himself is horrified by the very idea of the vodka martini, as he told me when I went to see him in Stockholm. It was with him, in fact, that I learned to drink vodka neat through entire meals: the end result is a marvelous clarity. He looks a little like the elderly Ibsen, with his pipe and his white goatee, and there is a durable quality to him, a meditative capacity for merry silence that seems to have been bred by the distillation process itself. For the Father of Absolut is an even, measured drinker, with the manners and voice of a chess player who occasionally likes a risqué joke on the side. I asked him how it felt to have invented the world's most universal alcoholic drink.

"It's not a bad vodka," he said. "But it's not a great vodka like my Gold."

"Did you think it would conquer the entire planet?"

"I think we were aiming to conquer Sweden mainly."

There seemed to be an element of repentance, of contrition, in his devotion to this small-scale, handcrafted vodka that would never make its way to the average hotel bars of Dubai. It was indigenous, introspective, a truly Swedish vodka that stood as a rebuke to all the two hundred vodka brands that come on the market every year.

Ekelund, too, that tireless alcohol tycoon, seemed a little embarrassed by the monumental success of Absolut. When I tasted his pure distillates at his farmhouse in Bjäre, he said that what had surprised him making Gold was the *greatness* of vodka when it respected its place of origin. Each sample of potato distillate did indeed taste different. Each year of Karlsson's Gold does indeed taste subtly but markedly different, yet this kind of discrimination has nothing to do with the success of vodka outside middle-class Sweden and upper-end bars in five or six cities elsewhere. People love to think they are discerning vodka drinkers, hence the success of the mediocre Grey Goose, which has marketed itself as a cut above other brands when it is nothing of the sort. Even James Bond, alas, mistakenly asserts that a grain vodka is invariably superior to a potato one.

"No," Ekelund admitted. "It's just a fashion. But what it's a fashion *for*, I am not sure. Absolut became a party drink. It became a drink for the young. Gay men."

Absolut carefully made itself hip to gay drinkers in the 1980s. But no one knows all the reasons why vodka itself became so indispensable. This water-ethanol mix became dominant worldwide in the last thirty years and has eclipsed Scotch, gin, and wine as a drink of choice by units sold and swallowed. It has become perhaps the most successful man-made drug of all time. It is surprising, to my mind, that is has not attracted a fatwa all for itself: the vodka fatwa.

Absolut, meanwhile, may have become a drink for the young, but I remember it as the drink of my Polish father-in-law, who died of cirrhosis of the liver in 1986. A writer convinced of the addictive evil of alcohol might have asked Ekelund and Karlsson about this, but Tomasz, I believe, had his own reasons for destroying himself, reasons that cannot be laid at the door of the two men who invented his drug. They did not, after all, invent vodka itself, let alone distilled alcohol. Tomasz was forty-four when he died, a brilliant violinist and conductor who had won the Koussevitzky Prize at Tanglewood and had been André Previn's understudy. At sixteen he had been the lead violinist of the Warsaw Philharmonic. The great Polish composer Pende-recki composed a concerto for him. He was a prodigy, a valuable asset of the Communist regime—and then he left for New York.

He was in his twenties when he emigrated to America with his wife, the singer Ewa Dubrowska, and their infant daughter, my ex-wife Karolina. They settled in New Jersey and then on campus at Ithaca, New York.

They were successful. She sang at the Met; he conducted all over the world. They got a place on Central Park West. He was a volatile, highly strung man, haunted by the Second World War. His family was from Kraków. When he was a small boy, he was picked up with his violinist father by the Germans on the streets of the city and transported to Auschwitz a few miles into the countryside. It was part of the random sweeps the Germans visited upon the local populations. Inside Auschwitz, however, his father was quickly recognized as a prominent violinist, and they were released. The Germans killed three million Catholic civilians in Poland, but on that day Tomasz and his father survived because they were not Jews. He never forgot it.

As his career ascended, he began to drink. Being Polish, it was vodka, but also Scotch. There were heartbreaking performances, one at Carnegie Hall, during which he lost his way in the score and his mind wandered. His career began to fall apart.

I met him first when he visited us in Paris in 1985, a year before his death and just after his grandson was born. He was jovial and mildly domineering, a scholar of the Second World War. He stayed with us two nights, and I noticed that he rose early and had worked his way through half a bottle of vodka or

Scotch by noon, sometimes a whole one. To drink late at night is one thing; to hit the bottle in the early morning is something else altogether. His hands would be shaking during lunch, his eyes watered down and wandering, as if turning inexorably inward. In such a sensitive and gifted man, it was an unnerving effect. He talked quite volubly, as alcoholics do, and his hand resting on the table in front of him seemed to vibrate. I thought at the time that a man's vodka addiction could be roundly regretted by those who surrounded him, but it was not exactly the subject of outright scandal. It was half-accepted, by law and by custom. And yet he was spiraling out of control.

I went with him one day to the Café Saint-Jean on the Place des Abbesses near our apartment in Montmartre and sat with him at a terrace table to have a get-to-know-you chat. We ordered drinks. I think he ordered a vodka tonic, and I ordered a demi. By the time I got past the foam at the top of the beer, he was on to a second vodka tonic. Halfway down the beer glass, and he was on to number four. "Don't worry," he said, "I can take it. I'm used to it." He wanted to know if I had any prospects as a writer and would be able to look after his daughter. None, I said. He ordered a fifth. By the time we walked back to the apartment, he was completely steady, able to walk in a straight line, and yet totally stoned. In the evening, he went through another half bottle neat.

Tomasz and Ewa separated, and Tomasz and his new mistress moved into a house in Ocean City, New Jersey, from where he took charge of the New Jersey Symphony Orchestra, based at Newark Cathedral. It was an ironic choice of abode: Ocean City is dry. Immortalized in Woody Allen's *Stardust Memories*, it replaces drink with ice cream, which is widely and freely available. There is not a single bar for miles around, unless you cross the proverbial railway tracks.

From Paris we heard stories of his accelerated drinking. Ewa died of breast cancer while living with us there, and after her death the stories of his drinking became alarming. His current girlfriend was unable to apply the brakes to him; terrified and baffled, she sent us back the reports of mad drinking sprees that lasted for days. During these sprees his mind would seem to take leave of his body. At the beginning of the summer, we finally received the call we had dreaded: incapacitated and dying of cirrhosis, Tomasz was in a hospital in Newark. We had hours to see him before he died.

We arrived at Newark with the baby and rushed from the airport to the hospital. It was over a hundred degrees: a heat wave. We arrived there just after midnight, exhausted. The staff at the hospital at first had no idea who he was. Then we were given a room number. I offered to go up first with the baby so that he could see his grandson before he died. Karolina was twenty that summer, barely an adult herself, and she had begun to realize that when he died, she would be orphaned in the world.

I went up in the elevator and exited into a long corridor of closed doors. His room was at the end. I knocked, and there was no answer. I pushed open the door, holding the baby, and went into a semidarkened room occupied at its center by a bed. In the bed was a shriveled old man with a dozen tubes stuck into him. I apologized and withdrew, then checked the room number again.

It was certainly the room number they had given me. I went
back in. It was Tomasz. The cirrhosis had made him literally
unrecognizable. High on morphine, he stared at me without any
idea who I was. I stepped closer and spoke to him, but he was
gone into his delirium.

He died half an hour later. Stunned, we went to the Manchester Hotel in Ocean City in a taxi. For the next few days
we went through his affairs, his large house filled with expensive clothes and musical scores. During the day we sat on the
sands of Ocean Beach and went to the ice cream parlors. We
ate ice cream because we couldn't drink, and we needed at that
moment to share a few drinks, which we could only do when
we went into New York for the evening. Otherwise we ate at
the Manchester and took the baby around Ocean Beach's gelato
joints. Sometimes, however, I went out by myself after eleven
and walked across the town as far as the railroad tracks hoping
against hope that I would stumble upon some hidden bar that
the town vigilantes had overlooked. But no—Ocean Beach is
as dry as a town in Saudi Arabia. I roamed through it with Tomasz's thirst, suddenly desperate for a drink. It was unthinkable
that he had chosen this place to live; but then again perhaps it
had not been entirely his own idea. A dry town for a wet man, a
cure for an addict.

My Sweet Islamabad

From Dubai, that spring, I flew alone to Islamabad. After the smooth ease of the Emirati city airports, their marble and technology, their generous space, the airport in the restless and dangerous city of Rawalpindi, Islamabad's sister town, felt atrophied and sad, surrounded at three in the morning by idlers and touts and men with heavy weapons. The road outside empty and half-lit, the taxi driver eager to get out of there as soon as his gas pedal would permit. A guesthouse in F-6, the safest and wealthiest quarter of the capital, a bare room with British fixtures, a smell of council house bathrooms, a terrace outside surrounded by the patios and windows of neighboring houses. A single house guard with an M15.

The days were sunny. Marmite fingers for breakfast and PG Tips with Carnation condensed milk. I could walk to the Great Mosque, that monument of 1960s taste that seems too big even for a mosque, and sit in the courtyards of white marble and be alone, untouchable almost.

I took a motorbike and rode out to Taxila, the Gandharan ruin in the hills north of the city, a Buddhist monastery patronized by Alexander the Great and destroyed by the White Huns in the sixth century. The guide took me around, astonished to see a white man on a bike, and pointed to the signs of fifteen-hundred-year-old fire.

"White Huns, sah. Here, White Huns." He shook his head with extreme but melancholic distaste. "Again White Huns, sah. Here"—pointing to hideous scaffolding—"*British*, sah."

The White Huns, the British, Alexander the Great. The Greek kings of the Gandharan era who minted their silver drachmas with images of both Buddha and Athena: Islam is only the most recent import into the ancient hills of Sind, subdued in the eighth century by the armies of nineteen-year-old Umayyad general Muhammad bin Qasim.

I went back to the city after these long trips to Taxila, and the city at night seemed secretive and withheld. Even at Hotspot, the ice cream place for the beautiful youth, there were men outside with weapons, and in the deserted restaurants there was a tension, an anticipation of unknown catastrophes. It was a place to savor life's inevitable solitude and uncertainty.

One night, nevertheless, tired of solitude, orange juice, and ice cream, I went to the Serena Hotel to meet a Pakistani businessman who had once been a friend of a friend in New York. The Dawat is by far the grandest restaurant in Islamabad, just as the Serena is the Pakistani capital's only true luxury hotel.

My guest, who insisted on anonymity, leaned over the table and whispered that the Afghan president, Hamid Karzai, was staying in one of the suites upstairs. "We might see him at dinner," he said. "We might be—alone with him." I looked around at a desolately empty room of considerable plushness. It didn't seem likely that Karzai would appear or that we would soon be enjoying a nice bottle of Bordeaux, though I was hopeful. I had heard that you could get a drink in the city's hotels, and not the fruit kind.

We were both in crumpled suits, awkwardly off-key. My guest, with the violently hennaed hair so disconcertingly popular among aging Pakistani men, talked in an unnecessary whisper. He wanted to know what I was doing in Islamabad. The country was hardly for the tourist trade, and he was pretty sure that I was not "an American operative." Certainly not CIA.

"I came," I said, also whispering, "to see if I could get drunk here."

He looked panicked. "Are you serious? Get drunk in Islamabad?"

I had heard that alcohol was so repressed now in Pakistan that getting drunk might be a cultural adventure all by itself. In one of the most dangerous and alcohol-hostile countries in the world, I wondered what it would be like to intoxicate oneself.

"You put that on your visa application?" he burst out.

I admitted that getting my visa in New York had certainly been an ordeal. Weeks of questions, delays, and paranoia inside the Pakistan embassy in D.C. Once when I called to inquire as to the status of my never-appearing visa, an employee had, after a polite altercation and a few expressions of frustration, screamed at me: "We don't have your passport! Go away now!"

My guest laughed.

"Yes, I see. They thought you were a visiting alcoholic."

"I am a visiting alcoholic," I said.

From a palatial marble lobby came the sound of a lonely pianist struggling with the simple tunes of *Love Story*, which echoed over and over through the Serena's glass-bright arcades and salons, which are lit with chandeliers but which never seem to fill. Seedy Americans sit in corners glued to their cell phones, also frantically whispering, also in crumpled suits, and a man in a red turban stands by the outer doors ready for trouble. They say the CIA are in fact fond of the place. Surprisingly, it hasn't been bombed yet, but terrorists are patient people.

With the rise of Islamic militancy, bars are obvious targets across the Muslim world, and for years, with grim fascination, I have been following the mass murder of humble tipplers in suicide attacks from Bali to Islamabad itself. When the Marriott Hotel in Pakistan's capital was destroyed by a suicide truck bomber on September 20, 2008, fifty-four people were killed and 266 were seriously injured. No one doubted that the Marriott's famous bar and its long-standing association with alcohol were one reason it was hit so viciously. In 2007 another suicide bomber had killed himself in a botched attack on the same hotel.

There is therefore an undeniable thrill about getting liquored up in Islamabad. The possibility is very real that as you sit discreetly sipping your Bulgarian merlot from a plastic bag, you will be instantly decapitated by a nail bomb. You might even be shot in the head for the simple crime of drinking. Your chances of dying in this way are not astronomically high. But nor are they astronomically low.

The girls in saris brought us our *haandi* curries with exquisitely tense expressions, and I asked Mr. A if I could suggest—it was just an idea, I'd heard it could be arranged—a glass of wine.

His eyes opened wide. "Glass of wine, *na*?"

I also whispered: "They can do it sometimes, no?"

"They can?"

He beckoned over a waitress and spoke with her in Urdu.

"Wine?" she said to me in English.

"Just a glass."

The businessman began to squirm a little.

The waitress, too, leaned in to whisper: "We cannot. Not even in a plastic bag. How about a fresh strawberry juice?"

"Watermelon, too, *na*," the businessman suggested hopefully. "They call it natural Viagra."

"All right." I sighed. "I'll take a fresh strawberry juice. On the rocks."

The waitress whispered even lower: "Sir, there is a bar downstairs. You can go after dinner."

"Bar?" the businessman hissed.

"Yes, sir. There is a bar. In the basement."

When she had gone, my friend frowned.

"It may be true. But it may not be true. I cannot come with you either way. They will never allow a Muslim in. I would be arrested."

I asked him what the punishment would be if he were caught sipping a Guinness with me in the Serena bar.

"It depends, *na*," he said glumly. "It could be prison."

"Prison?"

"Prison, sah, or a good thrashing."

Islamabad is the capital of a nation of 160 million people and is itself a city of about a million. And yet, my companion assured me, the number of places where you could get a drink could be numbered on the fingers of one hand. There were three open bars in the entire city, and only about sixty outlets for alcohol in the entire country. In the capital, aside from the secret basement bar of the Serena, there was a bar called Rumors in the Marriott Hotel. And there was reputedly a bar in the Best Western, though he had never been there. Outside the city, there was a luxury hotel in the hill station town of Murree called the Pearl Continental, where—again, according to rumor—there was a bar that enjoyed views of the snow-capped mountains of Kashmir. He had heard of a friend of his enjoying a gin and tonic there, *once upon a time*. There had also been a bar, he added, in Islamabad's alter-ego twin city, Rawalpindi, in a hotel gloriously named the Flashman. But the minister of tourism had vindictively closed it down.

The noose was tightening around the city's bar culture. There were bars of sorts inside some of the foreign embassies, but they were accessible only to the diplomatic corps. There was a UN Club, with access similarly restricted, and there was an Italian restaurant called Luna Caprese, popular with Westerners, where, as dark gossip had it, they would bring you a glass of wine from a bottle hidden inside a plastic bag. They wouldn't show you the label, but they would pour you a glass, and you would pay for it separately so that it didn't show up on the restaurant's books.

"Is it popular?" I asked.

He looked infinitely sad. "It was—until it was bombed."

After dinner my friend made a rather desperate gesture with his hand and walked off, wishing me a "pleasant drink."

I doubled back through the echoing arcades to a grand staircase near the Dawat that plunged down into an altogether different part of the hotel. There was not a soul there. I went down, slipping on the polished marble, and as I came into the immense underground gallery, a rather magnificent figure suddenly appeared, a bellboy of sorts done up in a beautiful white uniform with gloves and a turban.

"Where," I whispered, "is the bar?"

"Bar, sir? Bar is here."

And he executed a magnificent and regal flourish, indicating a pair of doors around the corner. I thanked him, and he bowed, moving with glacial elegance up the staircase. I looked around to make sure I was alone, a pervert approaching his darkest desire, and moved quickly up to the unmarked doors. I pushed the doors, and they merely rattled: the handles were tied together with a padlock. I shook them, but they didn't yield. It was not even nine p.m., and I realized that it was going to be a long night of strawberry juices.

. . .

A few nights later I went to the Marriott because I had a hankering for a gin and tonic, and it appeared that at nine p.m. it was the only bar in town that was dependably open. The hotel has now been completely rebuilt and is surrounded by soldiers and by those sad concrete barriers that you see all over Islamabad covered with stickers for Zic motor oil and a thing called Tasty. Inside, the Marriott lobby—garnished with fish tanks, Punjabi art, and box-shaped fountains—was nervously half alive; its opulent coffee shop was filled with Saudis planted stiffly in front of slabs of nonalcoholic cake. I went through to Jason's Steak House.

There was no one there. I ordered a steak and then asked, with my usual delicacy, if I could get a bottle of wine.

"I'll ask," the waiter said.

He came back with a black plastic bag with the top of a wine bottle sticking out of it. It was the red.

"And the white?"

"Not recommended, sir."

I asked what this one was.

He leaned down to whisper in my ear: "Greek Shiraz, sir."

The Marriott chain is a symbol of American imperialism across the Muslim world, but it was, as I have suggested, Rumors that had made this one so offensive to militants. This was the bar I repaired to after my steak and my rancid glass of Greek Shiraz. I was taken there by a bellboy. Down an immense lonely corridor, down a flight of stairs, turning left at a desolate landing with a lone chandelier, and down another flight of steps. At the bottom, like an S&M club buried under the sidewalk, was the neon for Rumors and the doors of the bar, shielded by security cameras designed to pick up errant Pakistanis. "This is bar," the boy whispered firmly, pointing up to the door. This time it opened.

I went in, expecting a riotous speakeasy filled with drunken CIA men and off-duty Marines perhaps abetted, I was hoping, by a smattering of loose Pakistani Hindu women. But no such luck. There was, as always, no one there. I took in the fabric walls, the fringed seats, the two pool tables, and the foosball, as well as the dartboard next to a plasma TV playing an episode of the British sitcom *EastEnders*. It was a very British and homey pub. A barman in a waistcoat stood at his post cleaning beer glasses and watching me with great interest. He was Muslim, and it took him little time to joyfully admit that he had never tasted the nectar of Satan even once.

He made a mean gin and tonic, however, and I asked him about the security cameras by the doors. He was happy to discuss them.

"We are catching those blighters every week," he muttered, shaking his head. "Muslims coming in for a drink. We see them on the screen, sir, so they cannot succeed."

Blighters?

"And what happens to them?"

"Ejecting, sir. We are ejecting. Sometimes police are called."

"Are the blighters thrashed?"

"Very much so, sir."

Alcohol has been banned for Muslims in Pakistan since 1977. A Muslim patron trying even to open the door of a hotel bar, as the barman intimated, will be asked for his ID, refused entry, and possibly prosecuted for the attempt to enter. Non-Muslim foreigners can enter, and so can the "unbeliever" 5 percent of the Pakistani population (Hindus, Parsis, Christians), who are asked to present both ID and a "permit book," in which their monthly permitted alcohol quota is registered. They are usually allowed six quarts of distilled liquor, or twenty bottles of beer, a month.

I asked him about the bombing in 2008.

"No one knows who did it. Osama bin Laden maybe. RDX bomb, sir." RDX packed with TNT and mortar.

"Are you afraid to work here?"

"No, sir." But his face said otherwise.

It was said that on the night of the bombing, thirty American Marines about to drop into Afghanistan were staying at the hotel, as well as an unspecified number of senior CIA officers. (A navy cryptologist named Matthew O'Bryant, working with the Navy Information Operations Command, was killed.) I looked down at the pulsating "stars" in the dance floor and wondered when that floor was last crowded with revelers. The barman said that in fact the bar was often full. Monday, he said proudly, was their busiest night.

"But," I said, "it's Monday night tonight."

A twitch. "Yes, sir."

"Is this really the busiest time of the week?"

"Most certainly."

At that moment the power went out. The barman lit a ghostly match, and we stared at each other across the bar in total darkness. Monday night at Islamabad's hottest spot. He managed a fatalistic smile.

Perhaps every bar now is a potential target. Nobody knows who masterminded that immense explosion that was heard miles away—Al Qaeda? an obscure group called Harkat-ul-Jihad-al-Islami? a group known as the Fedayeen Islam?—and no one ever will. U.S. officials have stated that they believe the bombing was masterminded by Usama al-Kini, Al Qaeda's operations chief in Pakistan, who was himself killed by a drone missile strike in January 2009.

In a sense, it doesn't matter. Modern 1960s Islamabad, Pakistan's Brasília, sits on the fault line of a lethal culture war. There were many reasons to hit the Marriott, but its association with booze was certainly one of them. Because not only does the Marriott house a famous bar, it also offers a curious Pakistani institution known as a "permit room."

A permit room is an unmarked liquor store sometimes tucked away at the back of a top-end hotel. Clients armed with a permit book or suitable foreigners can creep around to this secretive facility and buy bottles of vodka and Murree beer and then take them back to their rooms. The one at the Marriott is next to a laundry, around the corner from the main entrance. Surrounded as it is by sandbags and armed guards, you would never see it unless you were directed there explicitly. I've bought bottles of Scotch there, then had to do a kind of "walk of shame" as I hauled my boozy loot back to the main road, the Pakistani soldiers glaring at me with barely concealed sarcasm. It's like buying unwrapped pornography in a Walmart Supercenter in Salt Lake City.

As I sipped my over-iced gin and tonic and watched *East-Enders*, I recalled that Pakistan was not always hostile to drink. When it became independent after partition from India in 1947, it was still a country where alcohol was legal, as it had been under the British. Indeed the revered founding father of Pakistan—the British-educated lawyer Muhammad Ali Jinnah, known in Pakistan as Quaid-i-Azam or "Great Leader," who died in 1948—is widely thought to have drunk alcohol until he renounced it at the end of his life, though no books published in Pakistan may mention the fact or even suggest it as a rumor. (He was also reputed to eat pork.)

Alcohol was more or less freely sold and consumed from 1947 until 1977, when Prime Minister Zulfikar Ali Bhutto, eager to appease the country's religious leaders, outlawed it months before he was himself removed from power in a coup by General Zia ul-Haq.

Zia softened some of the original prohibition, allowing alcohol to be sold to non-Muslims, but the ban for Muslims stuck. The prescribed punishment for infringement was set at six months in prison. Pakistan suddenly went dry, and Zia's overall determination to Islamize Pakistan made that fact permanent. As Zia supported the mujahideen in Afghanistan during the Soviet occupation in the 1980s, a gradual conversion of the country from secular British common law to sharia religious law was set in motion by the American-backed dictator, who apart from privatizing much of the economy also instituted Islamic *hud* laws, whereby a person convicted of theft can have their hands and feet amputated. Alcohol would never return—officially.

For in reality alcohol pours illegally into Pakistan from all sides. It flows in from China and through the port of Karachi, bootleg vodka, gin, and Scotch that can be found ubiquitously in private homes and at private parties. "Bootleg wallahs" operate in all the big cities, plying the well-off with contraband liquor. Johnnie Walker, as everywhere in Asia, is as desirable a brand as Gucci, symbol of an entire way of life and consumed with the relish that we reserve for cocaine. The poor, meanwhile, gorge on moonshine.

In September 2007 more than forty people died in the slums of Karachi from drinking toxic homemade moonshine, an incident that scandalized the country. The producer of the lethal brew was a cop, as was one of the victims. The press wrung its hands, and legislators asked if the suppression of alcohol might not be connected to the rise of drug addiction in the young. A Treasury member called Ali Akbar Wains made the argument publicly after the parliamentary secretary for narcotics told the lower house of parliament that there were now four million addicts in the country. Parliamentary affairs minister Sher Afgan Niazi stated for the record, "It is a fact that restrictions in liquor have resulted in a surge in the use of deadly drugs in Pakistan." But the problem precisely is that alcohol is not just a drug.

It is a symbol of the West, a tool of Satan that denatures the true believer; it is also associated with sexual laxity, the mingling of men and women, and, one might say, the bar itself—a free public place quite distinct from the mosque or the bazaar, the two forms of public space that Muslim cities otherwise accommodate. Islamic radicals are right to hate and fear it. In bars, people leave their inhibitions behind.

A 2006 article in *Der Spiegel* put it bluntly: "The front line of the struggle against fundamentalism in Pakistan isn't in the mountainous border regions. It's in the country's permit rooms. Alcohol is sold there—and customers dream of the West."

Nowhere in Pakistan is this more evident than in the one place where it's legal to have a nip of Satanic distillate: the Murree Brewery in Rawalpindi. The brewery, for years the only one in Pakistan, was founded in 1860 by the British to produce beer for the troops stationed in Rawalpindi. Murree is high in the hills, and in the age before refrigeration, its location was ideal. With the coming of cooling technologies around 1910, the British moved it down to the hotter plains. Rawalpindi, meanwhile, became the headquarters of the Pakistan Army as well—and a sprawling, dangerous city filled with radicals. In December 2009 five suicide attackers stormed a mosque used by the Pakistan Army and shot dead thirty-seven retired and serving officers inside it. The Taliban claimed responsibility. To put it mildly, it's a bad neighborhood to be making beer and flavored vodka.

The Bhandara family, who are Parsis, took ownership of the brewery in 1961, when they bought majority shares in it. The present owner is Isphanyar, whose celebrated father Minoo ran the brewery for decades; Minoo, who died in 2008, was the brother of the noted novelist Bapsi Sidhwa, a remarkable writer afflicted by polio who wrote a beautiful book called *The Crow Eaters*, which I read years ago.

They are a cultured, literary family, and I supposed it was

because they were Parsis that they were allowed to run a plant
that produces a bewildering variety of drink. Aside from all the
vodkas and gins, they malt their own whisky as well as turning out Pakistan's most famous beer, Murree. The beer's logo is
known everywhere, even though only 5 percent of the population can drink it: "Drink and make Murree!"

Isphanyar is one of those youngish Pakistani go-getters
who never seem to be able to sit still for a moment, as if everything needs to be done instantly in case—for some mysterious
reason—it's too late. I met him in his office at the brewery,
where he sat restlessly behind a huge desk, blinking, pressing
buzzers and bells, and casting a watchful eye on the video security monitors. He wore a ring on each hand, a pink-striped
shirt, and a Rolex. The walls were hung with regimental British
Raj calendars with vignettes of mounted Hussars, and the desk
itself was dotted with garish little beer mats showing Pheasants
of Pakistan. A small desk sign read "Don't Quit."

In wall cases stood rows of Murree products: Kinoo Orange
Vodka, Citrus and Strawberry Gin, Vat No. 1 Whisky, clear rum,
and beers. There were also the fruit juices and fruit malts that
Murree sells to Muslims, foremost among them a thing called
Bigg Apple. When Isphanyar spoke rapidly on the phone, his
Urdu was mixed with urgently crisp English words: "maxi-
mize," "incentivize," "target," and then "look after him!" From
time to time he paused to sweep a deodorant stick into his arm-
pits and laughed a little nervously. He was handsome, quick, and
on edge.

I asked him if running a brewery in the world epicenter of
Islamic extremism bothered him. Or worse.

"Bothered?" he asked.

"Well, is it perilous for you?"

"All I can say is, we try to keep a low profile. I don't want my children to be kidnapped."

He pressed another buzzer. There was a whiff of Willy Wonka's Chocolate Factory, of delirious energy. "Strawberry juice?" he whispered into the intercom. "To Peshawar?"

He twiddled a pen and looked momentarily distracted as underlings came in and out, and I then observed that it was strange that a brewery in Pakistan could not sell anything to the vast bulk of the population; nor could it export. But this seemed self-evident to him.

"We cannot very well put 'Made in the Islamic Republic of Pakistan' on our bottles of vodka. But between you and me, the non-Muslims in this country are not the big drinkers. It's one of the ironies of Pakistan." He smiled cattily, and we were served a shot of Murree Whisky. To my surprise, it was excellent.

"What do you think?" he asked eagerly.

"It's very fine. Twenty-one years?"

"Our best. I will say, by the way, that it is *widely enjoyed* inside the country."

I had noticed that the brewery lies at the end of an unmarked track along an unmarked slip road, as invisible as such a large facility can be. It was protected by high walls and the usual armed guards. Ex-president Pervez Musharraf's house was nearby. It was like a town within a town, its dark red British brick, mostly from the 1940s, lending it a somber elegance of line. The air was thick with the sweetish smells of the whisky malting plant. As he led me outside, Isphanyar reflected on the volatility of the society to which he is, in effect, the leading supplier of a religiously outlawed intoxicant.

"The Muslim attitude is getting harder. Liquor, you see, is associated with a Western lifestyle, so it has become a flash point of some kind. Muslim hostility to the Western way of life finds its focus in alcohol. Hatred is directed at alcohol because it's a symbol of corruption. But at the same time the extremists tolerate beheadings, drugs, heroin, and kidnapping, and they grow poppies. It's bewildering, ah very. Do you not find it bewildering?"

"Very bewildering."

"We are most bewildered, I must say."

I was then taken around the malting and bottling plant. It's a self-contained production line: Baudin malt from Western Australia, Chinese bottling machines, Spanish labeling machines, cellars of Latin American oak casks that would not be out of place in Islay or Jerez. It was curious to watch the Muslim workers operating the machines as rows of Nip bottles of Vat No. 1 came pouring out. What was going through their minds? The foreman showing me around reminded me, as we strolled past whitewashed whisky casks, some of them dated 1987, that everything produced here had to be consumed inside the country. It was, to say the least, an enormous paradox. Five percent of 160 million is a fair number of drinkers, but I wondered if it could account for all these casks.

A little later in the day I went to a tasting of new vodkas that Murree is developing. The development meeting was attended by six staff members headed by Muhammad Javed, Murree's general manager, and each man gave the vodkas a score on a piece of paper. I joined in. Some of them were highly refined, with a soft "fruit" and a sense of serious purpose. Serious vodka, then, for a nation of serious drinkers? Javed explained that they were trying to develop vodkas even though their most popular drink was whisky. Vat No. 1 accounted for 40 percent of their total sales because it was relatively cheap. A bottle of twenty-one-year, on the other hand, cost about 2,500 rupees, in a country where the daily minimum wage was 230 rupees. Yet they couldn't make enough of it. Especially, he pointed out, when you considered that the government levied enormous taxes on it and they couldn't sell to the public except through permit rooms.

"Of course," he added, nodding with finite mischief to the others, "we all know that non-Muslims buy it for Muslims. A thriving trade."

My mouth rinsed with vodka, and quite tipsy, I staggered across the courtyard to visit Retired Major Sabih ur-Rehman, who was, as his card explained, Special Assistant to Chief Executive.

Rehman once participated in a study by the customs department that determined that about $10 million of drink was being confiscated every year, suggesting the presence of an enormous alcoholic black market. For every bottle confiscated, he told me, there were probably three in circulation. The study put the value of the alcoholic black market in Pakistan at about $30 million. This, he added, was driven by non-Muslims selling to Muslims. A bottle of Johnnie Walker Black Label cost about 1,200 rupees in an airport duty-free, but its black market value was closer to 5,000.

"Moreover," he went on, "the biggest bars in the world are the bars of Islamabad households, I can assure you. The bootleggers who deliver to your house are almost never prosecuted. The police protect them. Very powerful people run this."

He recalled that when he was in the army, they had bars called "wet clubs," though he wasn't sure if they still existed. Either way, he was sure that Pakistan was awash with booze, even if no one could admit it.

"I think people are drinking more, even if some figures show official consumption going down. We don't have alcoholism here per se. What we have is something else: it's that alcohol has glamour. It's desirable because it's forbidden fruit. That's the logic of human nature. By the way, did you try our Pineapple Vodka?"

What a shame, he implied, that they couldn't export it to the West.

"And before you leave, I'll give you a bottle of our whisky and some other things. Take it to a non-Muslim party if you're ever invited."

"Is it legal?"

His head jiggled, and he went all sly.

"Ah, legal—that I cannot say."

He smiled and jiggled his head again, and later, as I was driving back to F6 in Islamabad, I took out the beer, a bottle of Strawberry Gin, and a Gymkhana blended malt whisky they had given me and looked at the pretty labels. I felt like a heroin trafficker, though technically I was doing nothing illegal. I drank them alone in my room that night, sitting on a terrace filled with crows and listening to muezzins competing in the dark. It was, in a sense, like drinking alone at a bar when you have no one to talk to.

I tried the Strawberry Gin, assuming it would be too strange to stomach, and found instead that it was childishly comforting, well made, as if by people who knew its charms inside out. I would never have drunk it anywhere else. But it was a supremely delicious drink at that moment, and as I lay on my Spartan bed listening to the name of God ringing through empty streets, I felt a subtle intoxication reaching the ends of my fingers and the tip of my nose. A Pakistani fruit gin. What could be more seditious?

A week later my hennaed friend got me an invite to a private party not far from where I was staying in F6. I decided to bring my bottle of Gymkhana as a present, carefully disguised in a paper bag. The house of the affluent hosts—anxious as always about their anonymity—was one of the low, flat-roofed white villas surrounded by dry gardens and high walls that seem to make up most of Islamabad's housing stock. Inside, behind the discreet high doors and shutters, the house was filled with a mixture of Islamic art and reproduction Louis XV chairs, with cut-glass ashtrays and leather poufs and Kashmiri rugs. It was an older crowd dressed in Shetland sweaters and tailored shirts, businessmen and import-export men and their impeccable wives, and at one end of the long front room stood a little bar with a server in a bow tie. He was pouring out tumblers of Black Label and imported cognac, and the men were sipping from them as they sat in the Versailles chairs, assured that they were behind closed doors and that everyone knew everyone.

My friend asked me to relate the company a trip I had made to Murree the day before. I had driven myself two hours out of Islamabad to the old British hill station where the Murree brewery was started 150 years ago. I had visited the old brewery ruins, Victorian picturesque, and the abandoned British church, now surrounded by barbed wire, and finally the Pearl Continental Hotel, where I had had an eerie lunch overlooking the snowcaps of Kashmir.

"Is there still a bar there?" they asked.

Well, I said, that depends what you call a bar. After lunch I had asked the staff where the bar was—it was by now a familiar exercise—and they told me it was outside and on the ground floor next to the swimming pool. Off I went. After a half-hour search I eventually found an unmarked obscure door with a glass window that looked like a storage room. I knocked. A panicked face quickly appeared on the far side of the glass. We gestured to each other; me, upending a glass to my lips, he wagging his finger in a frantic negative. We pantomimed for some minutes. End result: no drink.

"Ah," they said, jiggling their heads, "we're glad there's still a bar at the Pearl Continental!"

They said it as if civilization had not yet fallen to the White Huns, and I had no idea what they meant. I opened my bottle of Gymkhana, observing that it was good to drink something local instead of the ubiquitous Black Label, and this was greeted with a chorus of approval.

We poured it out. It was not Murree's top whisky, but I thought it was a pretty good drink all the same. I noticed that everyone licked their lips contemplatively and stared down into their glasses for a moment. Was it a drink they knew so well that each bottle had to be savored for minute differences from the last one? Someone put some Rabbi Shergill (a Punjabi techno pop star) on the CD player, and soon half the room was dancing, some of the men holding their tumblers of Gymkhana aloft and twirling their women around. I recognized the song at once because it was a number-one hit in India, a beautiful techno rendering of a mystic Sufic poem by Bulleh Shah, the eighteenth-century Punjabi poet buried in Pakistan. Bulleh writes that he is "not the believer in the mosque," that he is neither Hindu nor Muslim nor Parsi, and that indeed he does not know who he is or what he is. Shergill's lyrical video of "Bulla Ki Jana" comes over as a plea for peace and tolerance in the Sufic spirit, strung along on the rhythms of global dance music.

"It reminds us," one of the women said, "that Pakistan was once a Hindu, a Buddhist, and a Sufi culture, and that all those things are still in us somewhere."

Did the Sufis drink? Did wine once flow through these parched hills when Bulleh Shah was alive? It was unclear. In the present moment, the alcohol seemed to have gently spread through the whole gathering, bringing everyone to life. A man waddled up to me and collapsed onto the same sofa. He was clearly mildly intoxicated, and he was enjoying it. He could say things that later he could disown.

"This country is fucked," he said simply in English, looking me dead in the eye and smiling. "We're going to be run by a bunch of clerics one day. We're going down the drain, down the drain."

I looked down and saw that the bottles on the coffee table were all empty. The barman was mixing cocktails—margaritas, as far as I could tell, with salted rims—and it was already long past midnight. The Koran had been forgotten, or shall we say revisited, and I picked out the strange words from the music, words after all written by a Muslim who had disavowed the religious orthodoxy of his day. They cut through the pessimism of the man who had fallen asleep beside me and seemed to move the hips of the people dancing to Rabbi Shergill:

Not in the holy Vedas, am I
Nor in opium, neither in wine
Not in the drunkard's craze
Neither awake, nor in a sleeping daze
Bulleh! to me, I am not known

Bars in a Man's Life

The term bar *was first used in* English in 1591 in Robert Greene's drama *A Notable Discovery of Coosnage.* Greene was England's first professional author and during his short life was known for a polemical attack on William Shakespeare. Did he invent "the bar"? The Victorians objected that the true bar was theirs. They claimed that Isambard Kingdom Brunel invented the bar to serve customers of his new railway at Swindon train station, or else that the Great Western Hotel at Paddington Station in London was where the first one opened. But either way, the bar is English.

A University Wit, a rake, and a drunkard, Greene was famous for his pointed red beard and for dying from a meal of Rhenish wine and pickled herring. His hilarious attack on Shakespeare is dead-on. He married a rich woman named Doll and spent all her money. He lived from scabrous pamphlets delighting in the seamier side of London and died as an indebted dandy. An allegorical image shows him sitting at his writing desk in his funeral shroud looking like a human turnip.

He was known in Elizabethan London for the *Coney-Catching* pamphlets, thinly veiled memoirs disguised as fiction, or vice versa, in which rakes and con men defrauded the upper classes to satisfy their vice habits. It was in this context that the word *bar* first arose. It was a new social space used by a new social class like Greene himself. A place to cheat, carouse, stand apart, boast, whore, and be left alone. But a place, also, in which a free society can conduct its informal business.

Greene is also said to be the model for Falstaff. In his death-bed book *A Groat's-Worth of Wit,* he wrote of himself that "his immeasurable drinking had made him the perfect Image of the Dropsy and the loathsome scourge of Lust tyrannized in his bones."

When I sit in Montero's in Brooklyn, once (and for more than a decade) my local bar, I think of Greene, dead at thirty-four of a pickled herring. I am in a place of his invention, or so I like to think. I, too, am the Image of the Dropsy.

This little stretch of Atlantic Avenue as it dips down toward the East River used to be the haunt of the longshoremen. Montero's is the last vestige of that time. The old feral New York has vanished, having served up to its progeny, like so many bad dishes, one difficult experience after another. The first years of arrival in New York were bad times for me, an age of poverty and crisis, but all the same Montero's was my bar during that icy age, and whenever I go through its door today (plumper and now armed with a credit card that works), I feel a slight panic, a regret for so much time wasted trying different kinds of Sauza tequila with the local drunks, all of whom are now dead:

characters who live on only in the unconscious of a sobered-up English exile who should have gone the same way as them.

One needs a bar almost as much as one needs oxygen, or shirts. Montero's was cheap and dangerous, and they served Vodka Cherry Bombs for three dollars. It is no doubt only a shadow of its former self. Its sign is red neon, hung above its door like something advertising cheap funerals. It seemed to be open all the time, which a bar should be. It was a dive with frills then. It looked like the boudoir of a disorganized Spanish madam. The women there were wonderful authentic sluts, a type that has been eradicated from the city by the police commissars who have so boldly improved all our lives by making our neighborhoods safe for Chihuahuas and homemakers.

There was a bell on the bar that bore a sign that read "Ring for merriment." Was Merriment a man armed with a cleaver? I never dared ring it, in case Merriment actually showed up. One looked through a bead curtain to the nether room where the pool table stood and where fights always began. The fights were very entertaining. They were squabbles over women and infidelities, and they usually ended under the pool table with a knife brandished at awkward angles by a man with no pants on. It had style of a kind, and the police were never called. There was a brothel upstairs, so they said.

Montero's was my local bar after I moved into State Street. The neighborhood was cheap and cheerily violent in those days. It was the Brooklyn of Paula Fox's *Desperate Characters.*

Montero's was often open at three in the morning, with men sitting perfectly motionless at the bar, their mouths hanging open. Heroin was also easy to score in the bodegas.

Even in the bar, the atmosphere was of imminent violence. The decorations encouraged it. There were clippers and schooners, with sextants on ledges and a cash register with little Central American flags. There was a photograph of a contortionist in the streets of Paris surrounded by trumpet players, and little B52s hanging from the ceiling on strings. Bullfight posters for Toros en Sada and the Great Manolete. There were pictures, too, of Joseph Curran, leader of the National Maritime Union from 1937 to 1973. A decor of anticipated intoxication.

In that place I encountered some hellish specimens, men pickled in Sauza and gherkin juice, with eyes colored by their own piss. Women drenched in some indefinable fluid, wild-eyed and smelling of cherries, with veins like nautical knots in their necks.

I found some drinkers who were legally blind. Blind as coots sitting there at the bar with a Cinzano and a cigar, night after night fading away and chewing cuds and following invariable baseball games through taped-up glasses. Every time I came in, there they were, as if they never moved, not even to sleep. I found myself on Schermerhorn every night, that suburb of Africa in those days, walking half dead past signs that read *Clean your blood,* past tenements cloaked in rotted ivy and Paco Jeans murals and Pioneer Warehouses with their stone scallops. There was no Atlantic Center then, just the old Temple Square fringed by check-cashing joints and gem pawnbrokers, with phantom

lettering suspended in the air around, spelling things like Tin-
ners Supplies and Gaswat Furnaces. It was a little corner of vital
hell unmodified by the gaunt mass of the Baptist church.

Montero's. I remember everything about that place. There was
a store called Dixon's next door selling ovens and gas meters and
a peritoneal dialysis center. There was a disabled veterans certificate in the window of the bar. The days of the Marine Square
Club, of which Joseph Montero had been a president, were all
but forgotten, sucked away into the past. There were life savers
above that bar, from ships like the *Houston* and the *Robert E.
Lee,* and a photograph of the old recreation pier at State Street.
That snapshot of the Parkway Hospital dinner-dance of 1951, in
which every woman looked elegant and beautiful—would that
be true now? Photos of Spain, of ships bordered with butterfly
wings, of flamenco dresses, and of Pilar Montero as a dancer
with castanets and the following bill for a long-forgotten event:

Gran Festival de Cante y Baile
Con la sensacional actuación de
Pilar Montero
Y su gran espectáculo
Rumbas, fandangas, dos orquestras!

I took all this in as my Drambuie drained away and my feet
felt cold. I enjoyed the fishing nets filled with conch shells and
the old wooden telephone booths. There were mounted antelope
horns, dusty sombreros, and old diving helmets hung next to a
small picture of a canal in\ Venice with a gondola busy being

predictably photogenic. From the 1950s, one might have said, like much else at Montero's, which seemed stuck in a midcentury time warp. The bar as a repository of the memories of ordinary people who will be forgotten.

The cities where one has lived through a life-and-death struggle always possess a vitality in the memory that the places associated with happiness and success can never have. I can walk down a few streets in a few other cities and feel a warm satisfaction, a desire to relive, but if I walk down Third Avenue in New York, for example, there will always be a bitter unease, a sudden ridiculous recall: one winter afternoon long ago I walked in and stole a huge Stilton from the Third Avenue Cheese Shop, a precursor of all the foodie stores now so prevalent in our city. Then, however, it was a novelty.

Down to five dollars and with no credit card, no family, no friends willing to lend any more, I walked in and decided the best way to steal a seven-pound Stilton was to be brazen. Just walk in, pick it up, and walk out with it. It worked. I lugged it home to Bond Street and rationed it with a teaspoon for four days running. Was I sober that day?

Even if they didn't want to lend me money for food, friends would always buy me a drink at a bar. It was entertainment for them. They could not, in any case, believe that a grown adult in possession of his faculties and living in one of the wealthiest cities in the world was actually hungry and didn't have the wherewithal to buy himself even a box of eggs. It was so amazing to them, so incredible, that they wanted to hear all about it. "Here," they would say, "have a fifteen-dollar cocktail, and tell me why you can't afford a pizza. You have to have a story."

But I didn't have a story. One falls on hard times in a foreign land, and it gets worse and worse, and soon one feels how a drinker feels as he descends downward through the social order while all his incredulous middle-class friends look on with disbelief and half-amused alarm. "It can't be happening," they say, and they believe themselves. But it can easily happen. You miss a rung on the ladder, and suddenly the ladder doesn't exist.

Later, those same friends would say, with obvious relief and a desire to clear things up a bit, "Well, of course, we knew you were drinking." It was their excuse for not quite believing it at the time, and their way of providing to me a conceptual framework for understanding such a near-disaster. I remember Quentin Crisp, who used to live around the corner off Second Street, and who sometimes came to Bond Street for tea, regal in his threadbare velvet hats, saying with grand and queenly authority: "If we got what we all deserved, we'd starve."

Coming from a man who lived in poverty, if more genteel poverty than mine, this seemed consolingly apt. One is responsible for one's own shipwrecks. Anecdotes mean nothing.

Still, looking back on this period, I cannot avoid asking myself if I really was drinking then but cannot remember it, or worse still if I refuse to remember it. It might have been a bacchic disorder after all.

In the winter of 1995 I stayed in a small Vermont village called East Dorset at a writers' colony. Having run out of money yet again (and in a place where credit was never extended in the single haute-bourgeois grocery store), I resorted to nocturnal sallies armed with a broomstick to knock down apples in all the gardens surrounding the writers' house—which itself was occupied by five lesbians from whom I could not cadge even a biscuit. Night after night I gorged on apples until the denuded trees drew attention to themselves and gossip began to circulate among the three hundred inhabitants of East Dorset. An apple thief was abroad. *Aux armes citoyens!*

It could not have been me, that mad and famished person cooking crumbles and tarts and pies every night in the small hours until the whole house smelled like an apple barn. But it was certainly me with the bottle of vodka I had obviously decided to spend my last twenty on, roaming around the moonlit roads singing to myself and abusing the dogs. The soles of my shoes had come away, I was in a tattered overcoat and a fur hat, but I was alive, and I had my bottle. Eventually, however, I was asked to leave. An old lady had spied me knocking down her apples one night: it simply wouldn't do, not among people dedicated to the finer points of creativity!

Onward, that winter, deepening into misery. On Thanksgiving Day I took a bus to Albany, the only person on it. I waited at the Albany bus station in a snowstorm and had the $6.99 Thanksgiving dinner, which I paid in quarters to considerable African-American amusement. By nightfall I was house-sitting in a ski lodge on top of a small mountain near Hunter, whence I had been taken by the four Albanians from Queens who rented it all winter for their skiing weekends.

How far can one fall while enjoying, in some strange way, the velocity occasioned by a failure of the parachute? Within days the chalet was snowed in. There was a bike on which to sail down to Hunter, where a lonely store stayed open till dusk. I took it one day, bought a half bottle of cooking brandy and some baked beans, and tried to cycle back up the frozen mountain.

By nightfall I had abandoned the bike and the cans of baked beans, which were later found by a family living by the road and returned to me. ("They was lying in the frozen river," the mother said, "like dead things.") There was nothing to eat in the house but cereal and condensed milk, but the addition of the brandy made for a meal. And then at ten, the other five lights on the top of the mountain shut down, and the dark night of the soul began. Wrapped in wool and blankets, alone with a glass and a great deal of time, I had, at that moment, little idea as to why exactly I was there.

In writing about drink, one is forced to acknowledge that its effects are never calculable or short term; nor are they the scripts that a taste for redemption and confession are liable to bequeath to us. Often it is just blankness, a nonbeing, a failure to show up for life during weeks and even months. I was rescued from my chalet existence by the appearance, one sparkling winter night, of the elderly architect who owned the land on which it was built and whose magnificent mansion—unnoticeably unlit so far—lay next door. He invited me round for dinner at once, with a flurry of "dear boys." In my rags, I stumbled over to his house like a medieval mendicant.

A fairy tale is never reassuring. Inside his house the architect stood with a little dog in front of cathedral windows, on the far side of which a waterfall plunged down between snow-white rocks. There was a table set with two places, a tall candle, and a bottle of burgundy. Would there be a price for drinking it and eating the food?

"Dear boy," he cried, seeing me, "I have everything ready. James is making us lamb roti with couscous. Sit. I have a bottle of Charmes. Let's make ourselves comfortable now, shall we? You look quite awful in that coat. Let's find you something better. And let's brush that long hair of yours. It's awfully pretty, but you've got it in a fearsome tangle. My, what a savage you are."

I think back to other bars in New York, where I spent most of my time when I could get a few dollars free—to the St. Regis Hotel, when someone else was paying, and to the places in Red Hook that I could reach with a long walk through the projects. The Liberty Heights Tap Room, delightfully estranged near Coffey Street, with its buildings that have the liver-red oxide color of Cambodian roads. I dream often enough of the Liberty Heights Tap Room as I lie in strange beds in strange cities, nostalgic for something I cannot put my finger on. A bar is like a second home, a refuge.

"The bar," as Luis Buñuel once wrote, "is an exercise in solitude. Above all else, it must be quiet, dark, very comfortable— and, contrary to modern mores, no music of any kind, no matter how faint. In sum, there should be no more than a dozen tables, and a clientele that doesn't like to talk."

How much time has been spent in these places? Years,

decades. Remembering them is like remembering faces. There are hundreds, and yet only a few are precious.

There is the bar at the Dukes Hotel in London, where they mix your dry martini from a trolley by your armchair. (I usually walk out from St. James's Place, cross over to Green Park, and collapse on the lawns.) I recall epic sessions with Mountbatten's nephew Michael Cunningham-Reid at the Mayfair casino in Nairobi while I was covering the murder trial of his friend Tom Cholmondeley during a long, exasperating winter: gin and tonic straight up, prostrate in the upstairs bar gazing up at murals of camels and men in pith. The colonial touch. An empire drowned in booze, the talk lapsing into incoherence. Lamentations that "nobody bloody drinks anymore." And who could exceed the splendor of the bar at the Muthaiga Country Club in that same city, or the cool whitewashed elegance of the Hope and Anchor in Phnom Penh, with its enormous fans and its bottles of DeKuyper.

Such places are scattered around the world, sanctuaries from the boredom of travel and the discipline of loneliness. Their ease and convenience can only remind of the terrible periods when their absence made life desperate. That winter on the mountain in Hunter, for example: for when the philanthropic architect had departed for his annual winter sojourn in the South of France, taking his largesse with him, and when I could no longer play the fool in exchange for a bottle of Chambolle-Musigny Les Charmes every other night, I was back to the distress that had confronted me just prior to raiding the Third Avenue Cheese Shop.

One night, when the snow was coming down and the

electricity was out, I thought that my benefactor would not mind it so much if I availed myself of one of his bottles from the cellar, so long as I left him a witty IOU. He would surely understand. Accordingly, I made my way in the darkness and tumultuous snow to his back door, where there was a cat flap at the bottom. Inserting my whole arm through this little aperture I could open the kitchen door itself and let myself in. It worked perfectly.

Rarely does one get to know how a burglar feels, entering another man's house and wandering through it in the dark, among the structured possessions and casual debris of an entire existence. It gives one a sense of filthy power. But I was not interested in voyeurism. I went straight down to the cellars where there was also a line of enormous freezer units. I found the wine racks easily enough and plucked out one, then two bottles of the Chambolle-Musigny Les Charmes. It would be for several hundred dollars, but I would write the witty IOU anyway. Then, as I was passing the freezers on my way out, I thought that since I had now incurred a debt of several hundred dollars, which I didn't and would never have, I might as well throw in a frozen turkey as well. If I was going to slake my thirst, I might as well deal with the hunger side of things as well.

Inside the freezers there were the largest frozen turkeys I have ever seen. One was graspable, but barely, and so I staggered back upstairs with the two bottles and the enormous glacial bird slipping constantly from one arm. I stumbled back out into the snowstorm and the impenetrable darkness and began to run gleefully back to my miserable shack. I daresay that I have never felt such a sense of personal triumph, such a complete lack of shame or moral compass. However, as I was sliding across a great expanse of frozen snow, the architect's security system suddenly sprang into vociferous life. Arc lamps cunningly mounted on the roof flashed on and a siren wailed across the mountaintop. Caught in the crosshairs of four beams, the thief was illuminated and transfixed.

My architect had once told me that his system was directly wired to the Hunter police station. And so, pursuing a drink, and because I could not do without, I barricaded myelf in my shack with a frozen turkey and two bottles of Chambolle-Musigny Les Charmes. Drenched in sweat, I hacked the bird into four pieces with a wood ax that the Albanians had marked with the instruction label FOR BEARS. I caught sight of myself for a moment in the mirror that hung in the front room: bare-chested, sweating, heaving an ax, and surrounded by shards of frozen turkey.

"Time to get a life, you sorry fuck!" I screamed at myself.

When silence and security had returned, however, and the police had still not come, I opened the first bottle of the '95. I drank it in a soup bowl. "Aromas still on the rise," I wrote in my witty IOU, which I later left under his doormat. "It's not a bad year at all, old chap."

Getting a Drink in a Civil War

Every man, woman, and child on earth drinks the equivalent of six liters of pure alcohol a year. The biggest drinkers, as far as I can tell, are the weary Moldovans, with eighteen liters a year, followed by the far less weary Czechs at sixteen. The Moldovans can rarely be sober, and in fact they should all be dead. But all the nations of the Eurasian northern hemisphere consume more than twelve liters, and according to various professional health bodies they should all be dead by now. The Balkans, though, drink less than the Finns; the Italians and Spanish are outdone by the Germans and the French. In Russia one in every five male deaths is by alcohol. Two and a half million people die every year, we are told, because of drink. Alcoholism is now classified as a "disease." It is like cancer or rabies. Its sufferers are helpless as its pathogens rage through their bodies; their sickness is passed on genetically from generation to generation.

Besides the toll it takes on the liver, there are aspects to this disease that can never show up in medical statistics. There is the yearning for conviviality, for the breakdown of a loneliness that otherwise cannot be so easily dodged. The transcending of the self. There is the unhappiness that comes with mundaneness, with normal life, which after all—and without undue exaggeration—leads to old age and death. So the departure from the self makes sense, and it's as easy as walking away from a mask and leaving it useless on the ground behind one.

The drinker is not adrift from normality because he wants to escape the mundane. He is the side effect of an insane belief that the mundane is all that there is. He is like the asylum inmate in Fellini's *Amarcord*, the mad uncle who climbs into a tree and refuses to come down, who beats his chest and shouts that after years in the asylum he wants a woman: *"Voglio una donna!"*

Yet stuck in that metaphorical tree, alone and frustrated, he will also want to climb down eventually. Terra firma beckons.

On the landing of the Pink Lady's eleventh floor in Hat Yai, seven Malaysian tourists, all men, stood among discarded drink trays, indolently looking down at their overpolished shoes. The landing was strewn with emptied vodka bottles, and there were little images of Thailand's King Bhumibol Adulyadej in white regalia pinned to the room doors. The walls shook with techno music. The Malaysians were waiting patiently for the elevator that would take them to the Relax Club downstairs.

Through a window spanned with chicken wire, we saw the

night vista of Hat Yai: rusted tin roofs, warehouses, a fragment of a decaying mosque with moss spreading along its walls. Expert punters, the Malays discussed the price of Black Label shots at the Pink Lady bar. It seemed like the shots were pricier than the girls, given that the girls could be had for about thirty dollars. I asked them, as we came into the Pink Lady's lobby, if they came here for booze or for the Thai girls. Booze with girls, they said with grim practicality. Why one without the other?

The lobby of the Pink Lady is not lacking in temperamental religiosity: grandfather clocks, mystical paintings of shrines in lakes, haloed Buddhas, and photomurals of saints. A talisman store stood next to two karaoke lounges, and girls floated past with trays of tequila and ice buckets. The Muslims seemed to find this mixture of religious kitsch and merry whoredom as irresistibly seductive as it was inconceivable. They blinked nervously. In the main hotel nightclub there was a "fishbowl," a seating area with benches raised like a small amphitheater, where numbered girls in togas awaited their customers, who merely had to call out her number to the mama-san. It's a familiar system in Asia. The painted background here was a scene of jungle ponds and shrubberies, a corner of a primeval forest. It looked like a panorama in an ancient Parisian zoo.

That night, however, there was only one Thai girl there. She was doing her knitting and didn't even look up. The Malaysians were disgusted and decided to go to the bar. We sat in the suffocating cocktail lounge and compared our phallic-shaped plastic room keys decorated with the words *Hot Pink*. I picked up some Malay sexual slang. "Cock" is *burung*, or "bird." "Pussy" is *nonok*. "Copping a feel, a grope" in the bars is known as *raba raba*. The noble act itself is *merodok*. It might come in handy one day.

They were professional white-collar types from Kota Bharu who had driven up together in a rented minivan, passing through the border at Sungai Kolok, a rancid village also famous for its liquored-up brothels. They were at the Pink Lady for the whole weekend, during which they expected to get laid at least five times apiece and to drink at least a whole bottle of Scotch each. That was not including the gin fizzes, the Royal Stag Indian whisky, the rum and Cokes, the Sex on the Beaches, and the Grey Goose shots *en masse*. The idea was to fuse sex and booze in ways that only a Buddhist country would permit.

"Then what?"

"Go home to Malaysia and sleep it off, la."

It seemed like a system. The cabaret started, and a few girls came prancing onto the stage in top hats and Moulin Rouge feathers. They held up gold amphorae to no effect. It was quite mysterious. The Malaysians seemed indifferent. They asked me instead what a *farang* like me was doing in Hat Yai, and I said I was traveling through the Deep South of Thailand in order to sample its nightlife. I was, in effect, traveling from Hat Yai to their own hometown of Kota, and I was doing it to see what made men like them tick. I was curious about the way they drank and the way they found their amusements. This made them roar with something that I took to be laughter, but that on second thought I was sure was its exact opposite.

.   .   .

It is sometimes hard to unravel the quasi-mystical workings of Thai politics, or to fathom why it is that this otherwise pleasure-driven nation should be plagued by the largest Islamic insurgency outside Iraq.

The Muslim insurgents of the Thai Deep South have never made intelligible demands, other than to evoke the possibility of a nostalgic resurrection of the Sultanate of Pattani. The Sultanate was a small Islamic state of prior centuries erased from the map when the British, then masters of Malaya, donated the three southern states to the Kingdom of Siam in 1909. The British, as no one now remembers, got trading rights from the Thais in return for the three hapless provinces. The Thais got a hundred years of fatal resentments, though they themselves had tried to dominate the region in the eighteenth century.

While the West has been focused on the recent political struggle in Bangkok, the longer struggle for the soul of Thailand has been evolving in the south. But the two are connected. Prime Minister Thaksin Shinawatra, ousted by a bloodless military coup in 2006, is the éminence grise behind the faction known in rather Dr. Seuss fashion as the Reds, who recently brought a near-revolution to the streets of downtown Bangkok. Before 2006, however, Thaksin was in charge of the war in the south. He took it personally. When the violence became savage, he took much of the blame for the army's reprisals against Muslims: the festering war may have done much to delegitimize, and ultimately fragment, his government.

No one really knows who the insurgents are, nor how many of them there are. For almost forty years up until 1998, a variety of guerrilla organizations operated in the south, committing sabotage, assassinations, and kidnappings in the name of creating a separate Muslim state. A group calling itself the BRN had formed in 1960 after the Thai government imposed a secular education system in the South. The BRN were anticapitalist, anticolonialist, and "Islamic socialist" in the manner of many movements in the Muslim world at that time, and they talked openly of rejoining Malaysia as part of a pan–Southeast Asian Malay-Muslim socialist union. They rejected the Thai constitution and proclaimed the supremacy of armed struggle.

By 1998 the Thais had suppressed the insurgency, but serious violence erupted once more in 2001 when Thaksin took power. He transferred security arrangements to the police, who are mistrusted and hated for their corruption; the insurgents meanwhile simply regrouped. By 2004 the violence escalated to sinister levels. Buddhist plantation workers and monks were shot, beheaded, machete'd to death. To this day the perpetrators remain, like criminal secret societies, eccentrically enigmatic: they include the Mujahideen Pattani Movement, PULO, and its military subgroups like the Ma-ae Tophien group and the ultra-violent Runda Kumpalan Kecil, or RKK.

In 2006 Wan Kadir Che Wan, the leader of Bersatu, one of the separatist groups, claimed to Al Jazeera television that the Indonesian terror network Jemaah Islamiyah was helping to launch violent attacks inside Thailand. It was the same group that bombed bars in Bali in 2002 and 2005, killing hundreds.

Now, as a Buddhist army occupies a Muslim land, the war seems ever more futile and obscurantist, more random in tone. It is, deep down, a cultural struggle with no possible resolution, an impasse that will never dissolve.

In the Pink Lady, meanwhile, my brothel punters were all too aware of the irony in their coming across the border to get away from sharia laws while the Thai Muslims were bombing everything in sight to get sharia law imposed in that same place. *Irony* is perhaps not quite the right word for dogged awareness of so ham-fisted a paradox. They pointed out, also, that even Hat Yai has had its share of malignant detonations. In 2006 bombs went off at the Ocean department store and at the Brown Sugar Pub, killing four. One of the dead was a Malaysian tourist, and one assumes he didn't enter Paradise. The scrofulous old *farangs* who used to come here for the girls got the message, but the Malaysians kept coming because they had nowhere else to go. It was their cheapest quick fix for sex and affordable Johnnie Walker. And what would they do without Johnnie Walker?

We drank it now with piles of off-tasting ice, and the men seemed to go into a state of catatonic contentment that derived as much from the brand name as from the alcohol itself. It was the partaking of a forbidden fruit, the quiet cocking a snoot at a taboo, a group transgression, and an escalating mind-alteration all at once. There is something undeniably fraternal about getting drunk in a group, particularly when the disciplines of family life and religious custom are absent. I asked one of them why drinking like this was so much better than boozing in their homes in Kota Bharu. "We not hiding inside," he said. "Total sharia almost in Kota, la."

Kota Bharu is in Kelantan, the easternmost state on the Thai border and the stronghold of Malaysia's most radical Islamic party, the Parti Islam se-Malaysia, the PAS. The party's leader, and the chief minister of the state, is Nik Aziz, who has pushed for full sharia law to be implemented. This includes amputation for theft and stoning for adultery: the standard civilities of *hud* law. The federal government has obstructed the outright imposition of sharia, but the PAS has won control of five of Malaysia's thirteen states.

I heard about the recent sensational case of the Malaysian model Kartika Sari Dewi Shukarno, who in 2009 was sentenced by a sharia court in the state of Pahang, one of the five PAS-controlled states, to six lashes of a cane for drinking a beer in a hotel bar. The sultan of Pahang commuted the sentence to community service the day before it was due to be executed, but had it been performed, it would have been the first judicial caning of a woman in modern Malaysian history. In February 2010 three women actually were caned for sex outside marriage, and most people think canings for drinking alcohol will now begin to rise as Islamization sweeps across the country. Drinking will become increasingly dangerous. Its allure will soar, and the border will boom.

Only half of Malaysia's twenty-six million people are Malay Muslims. The rest are Chinese and Indian and could not be covered by the laws anyway. "Islam is a soft, gentle religion," the redoubtable Nik Aziz has said. "We want sharia adopted across the country by consensus." Thailand, meanwhile, has the most radical Islamic state in Malaysia right on its border. It's both a curse and a grotesque business opportunity.

A few days later I took a private car from Hat Yai to Pattani. It's a two-hour drive to the coast, passing estuaries clogged with spike rushes, rice paddies, and orchards, the flimsy houses ringed with bamboo birdcages hung on strings: the ubiquitous, sad songbirds of the south. A hot, flat land with an exhausted lushness to it, a feeling of ebb and no flow.

Halfway to Pattani the road signs begin to be in Arabic script, and the first roadblocks appear. Thai Army units in their jungle camouflage helmets lounge under café parasols armed with M15s or sit with expressions of exasperation behind walls of sandbags. By five o'clock the roads are empty. After nightfall insurgent gangs roam them with opportunistic ferocity. Even at three in the afternoon my driver was eager to be off the highway. The minivans that are the usual transport between towns in the south have often been stopped, the travelers ordered out and shot on the spot. Local police stations have been hit with rocket-propelled grenades, and Buddhist roadside food stalls sprayed with automatic gunfire.

Few people come to Pattani now, though there's a sizable university, and its riverine neighborhoods of old Chinese shop houses used to draw Thai artists and bohemians. The city is under a hit-and-miss military curfew, and the only unrepulsive hotel is the now-ghostly CS, a mile out of town. It, too, was car-bombed (in 2008, two hotel employees killed) but was restored with Malay decor and Malay piped music; it now sits mostly empty at the end of a cul-de-sac behind armed guards, sandbags, and tired security cameras.

When I arrived, a few Muslim businessmen were on the outdoor terrace, drinking tea with Tea Pot brand condensed milk, the only thing served there. Tea, condensed milk, and sugar. With my cranky Thai I was able to persuade one of the hotel clerks to lend me his motorbike for cash. Taxis in Pattani are virtually nonexistent. They protested that it was suicidal for a *farang* to ride around on a bike, but it seemed a reasonable risk to get a cold Singha. Why would anyone shoot me anyway? It was Buddhists and other Muslims they hated.

I soon got lost, speeding through the Pattani hinterland, alongside the sleepy canals, warehouses, and rice paddies stilled within an unnerving calm. I was stopped by heavily armed Thai soldiers at a roadblock. They came out with their cameras to snap me astride the dirt bike, and I was high-fived: Buddhist recruits in complicity with the six-foot-five Englishman mistaken for an American. I asked them in Thai where the bars were, then how they felt to be posted here to Pattani, the most feared city in Southeast Asia, unable to even go to a bar when they were off duty. They were lackadaisical. The southerners were backward bastards, that was all. They were dying to get back to Bangkok for a weekend. We chatted about our favorites among the 120,000 watering holes in Bangkok, exchanging cigarettes, and I realized that our political complicity relative to the insurgents was centered on what the latter loathed most: drink.

That night there was a Chinese New Year festival in Pattani's old town. I rode there on the bike, through alleys where the lamps had been cut off, lit by overhead strings of red Chinese lanterns. A whole small city without neons, submerged in an atmosphere of latent violence and paranoia. Nocturnal running gun battles between police and insurgents are hardly uncommon in the streets of Pattani; nor are assassinations, executed with a chilling casualness from the backs of mopeds. Circling the town for an hour by myself, I didn't see a single night spot or bar, and not a single Malaysian tourist either. This is now by default an Islamic city that has stepped back from participation in modern Thailand. But the New Year festival had a rock concert and a dragon dance: I wandered through it with an iced litchi juice, while the girls in headscarves at the food stalls told me shyly that they didn't even stock Coke. Was it disdained in some way?

The Deep South does indeed feel like a place that has slipped away from modernity. The go-go bars, the obsession with technology, the raucous sex, and—perhaps above all—the relative freedom of women in the workplace? For Thai Muslims, one might say, it's Thai Buddhists with their easygoing tolerance who are "the West," the Dar Al Harb, the realm of infidels. The people who permit everything.

Back at the hotel, the lobby was a morgue, and the terrace

wasn't even serving Tea Pot. It was nine-thirty. I wandered out into the grubby plaza beyond the security barriers and noticed a rose-lit establishment of some kind where the usual Thai waitresses in slit dresses were lounging about at sticky tables. An astonishing sight. Sure enough, it was a modest one-room karaoke lounge of some kind, and I was able to order a Singha beer. It was clearly set up for Chinese businessmen staying at the CS or the occasional naughty Muslim willing to brave death, but there was no one there. I asked the girls where they were from. Unsurprisingly, they were Buddhists, some of them from the north, and they were uneasy working at perhaps the only bar in Pattani and so close to a hotel that had already been bombed. But business was business.

"The Chinese guys will come down bored out of their minds and order ten rounds of beer. The Muslim guys are like alcoholics. Drink, drink, drink. It's not our fault. We just hope they don't do a drive-by shooting on us. They love drive-by shootings down here."

They said it with contempt. They also said they had heard all the gossip being spread in Bangkok about the funding for the insurgents. Both local police and insurgents are suspected of being deeply involved in the drug trade. As in Pakistan, a country with four million drug addicts, narcotics are acceptable, but a sip of beer merits death.

Thais are also often convinced that the money comes from *tom yam kung* soup restaurants on the Malaysian side of the border. Since *tom yam kung* (a hot and sour clear soup with lemongrass, Kaffir lime leaves, and shrimp) is Thai cuisine's most recognizable tourist dish, that means a lot of restaurants funneling money for the terrorists. I had heard this same story many times myself in Bangkok, but these girls seemed totally convinced of its truth. Insidious soup sellers were fueling the beheading of Buddhist monks. It made them say cruel things about their Muslim cocitizens. It seemed so unfair, they said. *Tom yam kung* is a lovely soup, beloved of all patriotic Thais. The only thing harmful about it is its heat.

The following morning I walked into Pattani and bought a ticket for Narathiwat at one of the minivan transit companies. Narathiwat, two hours down the coast toward the Malaysian border, in the state of the same name, is another troubled Muslim city but with a much shorter history—it was founded only in 1936. It sits by a wide river and is known for its bellicose mosques. Ironically, the province's name is Sanskrit for "the dwelling of wise men." Eighteen percent of its population is Buddhist, and the more ardent Islamic persons wish them gone.

In April 2004 a group of thirty-two guerrillas in Narathiwat attacked a Thai Army outpost, killing two soldiers, then retreated to a sixteenth-century mosque named Krue Sae. After a seven-hour standoff, the Thai Army destroyed the mosque and killed all 122 people inside it. Thaksin was blamed by Thai liberals and reformists for excessive use of force. However, since 2006 the Thai government has been more conciliatory, apologizing for incidents like Krue Sae and promising to look into local grievances. This tone of contrition and apology, admirable in itself, has been greeted by the insurgents with an irresistible rise in violence. This has, to put it mildly, bewildered those who believe in the power of conciliation.

I fell in with one of the religious students who always seem to throng these collective vans moving from city to city. Hakim was studying in Yala and wanted to know if I could speak Arabic as well as Thai. No? He seemed mystified. He wanted to go study in Pakistan and, even more ambitiously, Saudi Arabia. We had a conversation about Islam's distaste for alcohol during the ride, and he made the delicate and sensible point that alcohol was forbidden by Islam because under its influence we are not "true to ourselves or our relationships."

Drink, in other words, distorts the individual's relationship to himself, or herself, and therefore our relationship to everything else. It was very like the conversation I had had in Solo in Java. Hakim was studiously compassionate and calm on this point.

"Have you ever drunk a drop?" I asked.

"Never."

"Then how do you know how bad it is?"

"The Koran has described it."

I said the Koran was quite vague on the issue.

Hakim did not see it with such equanimity.

"The ones who drink," he said, "should be flogged in public. What use is there for them?" Then, realizing that I might be some kind of Christian lush, he toned it down. "Of course, I mean the Muslims."

I asked him if he thought Kartika Sari Dewi Shukarno should have been caned for a sip of beer.

"Absolutely, absolutely. Was she not aware of the law? It's not important that it was just a sip. It's symbolic."

"Symbolic of what?"

"Of letting Satan into the picture!"

The minivans here take everyone to their front door, and our driver let Hakim off in front of a well-tended suburban house. He wished me luck in his "beautiful town" and gave me a friendly, masculine handshake that was intended to reassure me that nothing of what he had said was to be taken personally. Deep inside him, there seemed to be a dreadful innocence combined with a delicious sarcasm that was only half-conscious. Was he serious about whipping the Malaysian model?

I was dropped at the Imperial Hotel, the only habitable place in town. It was empty. The room was gloomy and bare with a black *qibla* arrow stuck to the ceiling indicating the position of Mecca. Nonalcoholic bottles filled the minibar, as accusatory as they always are, and the curtains smelled of thirty-year-old cigars. I didn't mind. I went out for a walk after dark, as the loudspeakers from the mosques began to bray. In hotels like this, one is always forced out onto the street sooner or later.

The Friday-night sermon in the mosque across from the hotel was in Yawi, the variant of Malay spoken in the south, and after every furious phrase, the imam paused and sighed a long, exasperated *aaah*. Men stripped to the waist in the cafés, watching Manchester United games with plastic mugs of litchi juice mixed with green gelatin, paused between goal kicks to lend an ear, and the boys lounging on their motorbikes by the river glanced up as the *aaah* echoed across the night.

I failed to find a single outlet for alcoholic pleasures and, defeated, slogged back to the Imperial and the prospect of a long night of orange juice and Malaysian Koranic TV. As I was going through armed security, however, I saw a tall *kathoy* or "ladyboy" (technically a hermaphrodite, but usually a man who has had surgery) clattering across the plaza. When in joyful hedonistic Narathiwat, I thought to myself, always follow a ladyboy. She went to a "saloon" that I had not noticed earlier.

The saloon, however, only contained the ladyboy, and she looked at me shyly before asking me what I wanted. It was a good question. I had the feeling then that asking for sex with a transsexual hooker might be less dangerous than asking for a Stella Artois, and the transsexual hooker knew it. She confronted me playfully along these lines, and I stuck my neck out and ventured for the beer. She went into a back room and came back with a Chaang, a local brew, and then turned on the karaoke screens. I had to be entertained.

"Me and you?" she finally said in English, turning a long painted fingernail upon herself, and then upon me.

Refusing gallantly, I asked her if drinking a Chaang was safe. Those *aaah* sounds coming from the mosque did not sound friendly.

"No," she said in Thai. "He is talking about the importance of washing. Washing your feet."

"Nothing about drinking?"

"That was last week."

What about ladyboys, I wanted to ask. *What does the Koran say about them?*

It's a sad fact that life by and large would be endurable, as Sir George Cornewall Lewis once said, were it not for all the pleasure we have to endure. That night I had a nightmare and woke up convinced that, as far as I could see, a giant beetle was walking across the ceiling. It was, however, the humble *qibla.* In the morning, either way, they politely and apologetically informed me that a bomb had gone off in Narathiwat the previous day. No one seemed particularly surprised, but a generalizing, cosmic apology was nevertheless offered.

I rode in another minivan down to the Malaysian border, to the raffish and unstable town of Sungai Kolok, which sits insalubriously along a narrow river (*sungai* in Malay means "river") that is, in effect, the border. How sweet life would be if one could, at all costs, avoid Sungai Kolok. One could grow old and happy and hale without Sungai Kolok.

It is here that most Malaysians furtively come when they need a break from the sharia regime of Kelantan, and there are special all-in-one hotel brothels that cater to their urgent and time-constrained needs. Chief of these is the Chinese-style Genting Hotel, named for the hill region of Malaysia where the British once had their charming stations. The Genting is only a hundred meters from the border, and you can walk if you don't mind the heat. You can pay here in Malaysian ringgit, and the second-floor cabaret and lounge is a source of local girls who eagerly await the flow of Muslim men. Frequent bombings and shootings in Kolok have only temporarily dampened their ardor, and it is remarkable what men will brave to get laid and to sip a tumbler of Sang Thip whisky, preferably at the same time.

The Genting specializes in dance parties, and that night one of them was in full swing. Unlike the Pink Lady, the Genting is also a merry family hotel, and its restaurant doubles as a night-club where six-year-old children dance between the tables to wildly out-of-tune middle-aged Thai crooners singing *luuk kru-ung* country music ballads. The girls from upstairs sit around in their fringed white boots holding teddy bears and halved pineapples, eating dishes of *kaeng som,* and among them move the slightly uncertain, slightly tense Malaysian visitors who never seem to smile and whose eyes look subtly hunted. It's a ragbag crowd, and there is nothing very louche about it. Even the massage parlor upstairs seems laid back and wonderfully unrepentant.

At the bar next to it, I sat talking to a sixty-year-old engineer from Kota who said he had just scored a cut-price haul of *kanagra,* the generic Thai version of Viagra that retails for about five dollars for a blister pack of four. He had a glass of Mekong Scotch on the bar, and the girls were telling him not to drink the fearsome Mekong and take *kanagra* at the same time. He was tiny, bald, and slipping off his stool. His name was Yussef. He was protesting that the symbiosis of *kanagra* and Mekong was perfect bliss.

"You bad man," they said in English. "You come here boum-boum lady. You die heart attack."

"Wonderful ladies, la," he said turning to me. "So graceful."

"I'll buy you a drink," I said. "Mekong again?"

We talked about Kolok. It was a fine enough hellhole, he said in English, thinking the girls wouldn't understand, but the insurgents liked bombing it, perhaps because they thought it was a haunt of Satan.

Wasn't that a little ironic, I asked, given that it was a Muslim town filled with Malaysian tourists?

"Yes, but we are sinners to be here in their eyes. We deserve to be killed with shrapnel."

"Are you their ideal target then?"

"I am not sure they are trying to kill Malaysians. They are trying to intimidate the Thais. But many Malaysians have been injured by bombs in this town. It's a tiny town, too." He smiled. "They can't miss us."

The bombings of coffee shops, bars, and ATM machines had indeed mutilated a fair number of Malaysians. Yet still they came.

At night, though, most of Kolok was quiet, and the trees in February swarmed with thousands of chattering birds that yielded its only nocturnal sound. The streets were deserted after the food stalls closed down, and it was only the hotels and their surrounding dives that seemed to remain alive. The Marina, the Sum Time Bar, the Tara, which housed the Narcissus massage parlor, the Mona Lisa Massage at the Marina, which sported a large image of Leonardo's dame with bared breasts. Downstairs at the same hotel the Malaysian men crowded around the plasma TV to watch English Premier League games. "Liverpool!" they cried, as if in anguish, raising their fists. The Chinese temples, on the other hand, and the lanes of red lanterns and metal shutters remained darkened. The pendant birdcages had their birds removed. There was a strange charm to the place. The mixture of Chinese, Thai Buddhists, and Muslims was not dead or fossilized. It was the public space of the hotel, however, that kept it humming after hours, even if none of the bars appeared to be open.

I got up early to get some cash from a nearby ATM machine and had breakfast at the Genting: Nescafé, oranges, and congee. I was joined by some of the Kota sex tourists who insisted on recounting their conquests of the prior night. They seemed immensely pleased with themselves and were going back to Kota with a measure of decent, glowing satisfaction that needed an audience. Super Premium model good, la?

I listened to them dutifully and then left the hotel a few minutes later. As I walked through the windless heat to the ATM machine, I noticed that the street seemed uncommonly deserted. It was about eight a.m. Suddenly there was an ear-splitting detonation, and a puff of smoke appeared above the roofs. When I got to the ATM machine, it had been atomized by a small bomb. The local police later identified the culprits as members of the RKK insurgent group, headed by the splendidly named Wae-ali Copter Waji.

As I took a taxi across the border to Kota Bharu after lunch, I pondered the inherent glamour of being murdered by Wae-ali

Copter Waji for the sin of using an ATM machine. Would Mr. Copter slay me, too, for watering my lips with fermented barley?

I wanted to see Kota at long last because it seemed to me that in some way it was a version of what the insurgents in Thailand were fighting for: a sharia way of life, at least partially; an Islamic city free of the scourges they associated with the corruptions of Thailand. Not only no girlie bars, but no bars period. I also wanted to see where Malaysian sex tourists came from.

Nik Aziz's capital, as it turned out, was a pleasant city. It was calm, orderly, and mild, with air-conditioned malls like the KB Trade Centre, little red phone boxes with the word *Helo* written on them, branches of EONCap Islamic Bank, and neoclassic cream-white emporiums dating from the British 1930s like the Bangunan Mawar. It was a much nicer city than Sungai Kolok or Hat Yai. It was cleaner, more salubrious, more familial. I saw signs for Frost Rut Bir but, as expected, no vestiges of nocturnal social life. I had expected a version of Tehran, or even worse, a dark and dingy pile terrorized by loudspeakers, and lo, it was more like Elizabeth, New Jersey, a slice of imitation America influenced perhaps by the aspirations of Singapore.

As the sun fell and dusk came on, the mosques sprang to crackling life, but the streets began to die. Between the mosque and the mall—our version of the souk—there was nothing but domesticity, a guarded privacy. The city was closed against outsiders, against visitors. While Malaysians flocked to Thai cities, clearly no Thais ever came here.

Roger Scruton, in his book *The West and the Rest,* has described this bipolarity of the traditional Islamic city:

> The mosque and its school, or *madrasah,* together with the *souq* or bazaar, are the only genuine public spaces in traditional Muslim towns. The street is a lane among private houses, which lie along it and across it in a disorderly jumble of inward-turning courtyards. The Muslim city is a creation of the *shar'ia*—a hive of private spaces, built cell on cell.

But is Kota such a traditional city? That may be what it increasingly aspires to be, but it is also a place where the malls are chilled and the infidel brands proliferate merrily enough. It is certainly comforting, provincial, domestic. One misses at once the garish, insolent public space that is the bar. An idle reflection: if a town cannot have opera houses, theaters, art galleries, or sports stadiums, the bar is the simplest, the most universal, and the most accessible public space. As I walked through Kota's delicate quiet, under its trees heavy with birds, I thought nostalgically—but also incredulously—of the scores of mobile bars that line Sukhumvit Road in Bangkok every night, little more than motorized wheelbarrows that appear at dusk and are mysteriously driven away at dawn. It's a brilliant concept: a temporary occupation of a piece of sidewalk, a row of vodka and Scotch bottles, a line of chairs open to any stranger. It's part of what makes Bangkok feel so free in its earthy, immediate, open-to-all way, and I've noticed that the mobile bars are much loved by visiting Malaysians, Arabs, and Iranians. But they are not here and never will be.

It is not just the booze and the loose women, however, that draw the men of Kota north of the border. It's public spaces where anything can be said without fear of misappropriation. The things that cannot be said in the mosque or at home, in other words—the humble subversions of the spoken word that have been lubricated by alcohol. Or set free by it. In the West the bar began as the coffee shop and café in eighteenth-century London and Paris—it is where modern politics was born. Its absence in a large town or city strikes one as a repudiation of sorts, a turning back. Though it is a repudiation that is not without its reasons or its charms.

Kota was the first place in the region I visited that did not live in daily fear of assassinations and bombings. Perhaps the absence of any trappings of contemporary urban life was the reason. The Islamic warriors did not see anything to enrage them. The bar did not exist. The women were not "exposed." There was just the mall, where I sat down at last to eat an ice cream under the smiles of the headscarfed girls who served them. Ice cream. Isn't ice cream always the substitution for a nice beer, from dry Islamabad to dry Ocean City, New Jersey? A good ice cream lulls the mind in the same way, almost, and there is about it the sweet intoxication of virtue.

Usquebaugh

Often when I am in a bar in the East—at the bar on top of the Baiyoke Tower in Bangkok, for example, whose exterior skyscraper is draped with a vast image of a striding Johnnie Walker—I will think back to days spent on the island of Islay in the Inner Hebrides.

Scotch has a special place in the Asian heart, and for that matter in the heart of virtually every non-Western country. It is a strange drink for the world to have adopted so vigorously. Its appeal is a mystery. The obsession with Johnnie Walker, for example—that fetish brew that is without fail produced after dinner at affable and affluent tables from Cairo to Seoul to Bombay. Status, refined manliness, colonial-officer-class panache— all are rolled into the amber fluid. And while Johnnie Walker is the preferred whisky of palateless businessmen all over the East, the more refined single malts of Islay and elsewhere have also begun to make their way into the haughtier bars. The affair with whisky is only beginning.

Islay. It's a place I used to visit to pick up odd bottles and to explore, to lose myself for a few days. And in fact Islay has always drawn me to her. I used to go there in the early summer, when the winds abated a little, to walk about like a penitent with my umbrella and my *Whisky Bible*, alone and subtly distraught, abstemious on many fronts but thirsty for a new Scotch I didn't yet know. I took buses in storms of salted rain to distilleries as white and pure and remote as monasteries. It was like Greece in winter.

As with wine, a drink cannot be understood without seeing where it comes from: here, a speck of peat in the Atlantic a forty-minute plane ride from Glasgow. A place as remote from Bangkok or Tokyo as you could imagine. Yet the threads of a thousand and one drinkers bind these places together. In Japan, Islay is more known than Budapest, Kiev, or Glasgow.

Islay is a landing strip in the ocean. It is only thirty miles by thirty, with a population of three thousand and an airport that looks like a gardening shed. Does the rain seep into Islay's whisky, too? When does it not rain on desolately weird Islay? So it seems, as you make your way past Morag's Caf, an airport lounge glittering with display bottles of local single malts. You step out of the airport into *Wuthering Heights*.

The bartenders, sent all the way from Tokyo to learn about Islay malts, wear a look of dismay as they clutch their Burberry raincoats and venture outside into those unforgiving gales. Everything is slanted, horizontal, wind-bent. "A bonny day!" the craggy locals cry at them. Across from Islay lies the island of Jura, inhabited mostly by deer, and from here comes the humble but supple Jura malt.

I drink Jura in New York at the Bridge Café on Water Street; it's the oldest bar in the city and a temple to the single malt, stocked in ten- and fifteen-year editions. To sit on Water Street, in a designer mall where history has been rekitted for urban tourists, and sip Jura fifteen-year single malt is to be saved for half an hour. There are Scotches like this, delicate and brooding at the same time; Dalwhinnie and old Port Ellen, which Diageo now puts into its Johnnie Walker Blue Label, or Talisker's Anniversary Edition. I used to go to the Scotch tastings held by master distiller Evan Cattanach of the Classic Malts Collection. They were held in the Chairman's Office room inside the Palace Hotel on Madison and East 50th Street, that bustling grand dame hotel that no one seems to go to for a drink. Scotch dinners at which rare malts were served with seven courses, Evan dressed in a kilt and courting the ladies and digging into his reserves to make us taste twenty-five-year Brora, the loveliest of all single malts made by a distillery on the wild east coast that no longer exists. Here was the place to take old Islay malts, served at the end of the meal, the quarter-century editions of Lagavulin and Laphroaig and the occasional Caol Ila and Ardbeg. During Prohibition, Islay malts were the only liquor you could legally buy in the United States. Their iodine content was so high, they could be sold as medicine in pharmacies.

On the Islay municipal bus that runs between Bowmore and Ardbeg, you pass along the southern coast road through peat heaths, crofts of twisted trees. The two distilleries sitting side by side like the seafront castles of rival clans—Laphroaig and Lagavulin—have their whitewashed walls built right on the water. The black letters of their names are written across

them, making for photo ops that the Japanese have captured a
million times.

On the headland by Laphroaig stands the actual ruined castle
of the Lords of the Isles; I was shown around Laphroaig—which
means "beautiful hollow by the broad bay" in Gaelic—by its
master distiller, John Campbell. We went up to the cement-
floored malting room, where Laphroaig's barley is rolled out
and dried. Malting is the process of flushing barley three times
with water to make it germinate over a period of fifty-two hours.
The husks are then dried three times as well. Laphroaig is one
of only five distilleries in Scotland that "floor malts" by hand—
that is, they expose the grain to natural air by opening and closing windows. Enzymes pour through the tiny acrospire at the
barley husk's core, and at its tip an embryo begins to emerge.
Campbell split one and showed it to me, adding that this means
the barley is getting ready to produce sugars. But before this
germination actually occurs, there's an intermediate step: the
husks are shoveled into a kiln room for the process known as
peating. A peat fire belches a perfumed smoke into the kiln for
fifteen hours and saturates the dried-out barley with its aromas.

Laphroaig peats intensely. Most Scotches are said by con-
noisseurs to boast half a dozen smoke flavors, while Laphroaig
yields at least fourteen. Laphroaig's seaweedy taste comes solely
from the peat. But this makes sense: Islay's peat is formed from
iodine-rich seaweed, while Highland peat comes from wood.

Whisky's amber color, however, comes from cask wood and
nothing else: usually either old recycled Bourbon barrels or
sherry vats from Spain. The former produce a lighter potion,

the latter a richer, darker Scotch. Ian Hunter, the legendary owner of Laphroaig until 1952, scoured the West Indies for rum vats that would give soft aromatics of banana and coconut, and I have often noticed in older Laphroaigs—a sixteen-year-old, for example, has a subtle taste of orange rind and lemon—a whiff of subtropical sun. Mysteries of the "water of life," then, whose background odors are not entirely of the North. The Islay malt, lightly diluted by a single cube of ice (which is too much), is southern and Mediterranean as well. It has a dry heat in it. It is a *whisky di meditazione* that puts the drinker in a perilous relation with his own morbidity.

The Irish, I am bound to admit, have a particular penchant for this relation between intoxication and morbidity. "I have absolutely no pleasure," Edgar Allan Poe once wrote, "in the stimulants in which I sometimes so madly indulge. It has not been in the pursuit of pleasure that I have periled life and reputation and reason. It has been the desperate attempt to escape from torturing memories, from a sense of insupportable loneliness and a dread of some strange impending doom."

Poe may not have been Irish and he may not have been talking about whisky, but this is also the hard drinker's paradox. The pleasure of what he drinks is not exactly why he drinks, and the pleasure of Scotch is not entirely gustatory. It is a difficult, thorny drink, and it is hard to see how the Plains Indians of the nineteenth century became so addicted to it without the psychological dimension described by Poe. It sucked them, and

us, into its moods and not just into taste sensations. It destabilized them into madness, into altered states of melancholic
strangeness, and ultimately of course it destroyed them.

The writer Niels Winther Braroe wrote in *Indian and White*, a
1975 book on Indian-white relations, that "drinking is one of the
faults that Whites most frequently single out in censuring Indians, and every Indian is aware of this. Indeed, it is expressed to
them by Whites in numerous contexts—sometimes contemptu-
ously and sometimes sympathetically, in subtle and not so subtle
ways." The Indian reservation habit of "going on a toot" (that
is, a bender) is part of non-Indian lore. Like the Irishman, the
Indian is a *congenital drunk*.

An article in *Time* from March 1932, from the town of Globe,
Arizona: the murder trial of twenty-one-year-old Apache Seymour, sentenced to life in prison for the rape and murder of Co-
lumbia ethnology student Henrietta Schmerler, a protégée of
Ruth Benedict, on the White River Reservation. Seymour had
been drinking tulapai, identified quaintly in the article as "ab-
original moonshine." The white girl stopped him on his horse,
he said, invited him inside her house, gave him another drink,
and began to kiss him; they got on a horse together, and there
was a struggle, a fatal misunderstanding, a sexual dance gone
wrong, a killing with a rock. The defense attorney said to the
jury, "I propose to remind this court what is known to everyone
here—that tulapai to an Apache is murder."

.   .   .

Prior to the arrival of Europeans, the Plains Indians had no experience with mind-altering intoxicants of any kind. In this they were unlike the nations of the Southwest, like the Apache, who made an alcoholic drink similar to the mescal-like *sotol* out of a plant called *Dasylirion wheeleri*, or the Tohono O'odham of southern Arizona, who made a fermented saguaro cactus drink called *tiswin* that was used ritually. Intoxicants were part of the initiation rituals of young girls among the Apache.

But in the north it was different. Alcohol appeared on the Great Plains only between 1790 and 1830, with the arrival of European traders on the Missouri River. The Plains Sioux were anciently dry. Distillations, like the horse, transformed them.

The brandy of the French and the rum of the British had always been the handmaidens of the fur trade, and as the taste for alcohol evolved among the indigenous nations, so did their inclination to trade their precious furs for drink—a substance that yielded no economic benefit to them whatsoever. Fur, rum, and brandy—and then whisky—were the mediums through which Amerindians and Europeans conducted their calamitous exchanges, and in a study of the effect of alcohol on the Lakota, the activist Beatrice Medicine makes the case that alcohol was a conscious weapon of colonization. "Used as a potent item of trade," she writes, "alcohol was effective in gaining furs, food, women and land for European interests."

Congress nevertheless restricted the sale of alcohol to Indians in a law of 1802. After the War of 1812, however, John Jacob Astor's American Fur Company arrived in Sioux lands, and the fur-alcohol symbiosis unleashed an epidemic of alcoholism. The company kept its own liquor stock for Indian trade, the whisky often adulterated with laudanum, a tincture of opium. The laudanum supposedly sedated the Indians and made them less inclined to murder one another while drunk. The whisky was often offered free to the Sioux hands, to lure them away from rival fur companies, though by the 1840s the trade had waned. Whisky had become expensive for Indians, and the government's ban had begun to come into effect. On the east banks of the Missouri, however, so-called whisky ranches carried on the barter trade: booze for furs and clothes. Many Lakota stripped their families to the bone for a bottle of "tarantula juice." The illegal whisky trade flourished. The distillate of a small Celtic corner of the British Isles became the destroyer of entire nations of North America.

The reservations, though, became dry. The Pine Ridge Reservation of the Oglala Lakota has been dry since it was created in the 1880s. Its thirty thousand inhabitants have among the highest rates of alcoholism in the world, but they have to drive two miles south of Pine Ridge to the tiny village of White Clay to buy their liquor. White Clay is little more than a stretch of road with a few shacks on either side of it. It has a population of eleven and four liquor stores selling four and a half million cans of beer a year. It lies in what was once known as the White Clay Extension, a kind of buffer zone set up by President Chester A. Arthur in 1882 to protect the Oglala from illegal whisky traders. Until the two bars in White Clay were permitted on-sale consumption of alcohol in the 1950s, White Clay was a bootlegger town servicing the Oglala addiction. Today it does the same, but with beer. The town becomes a camping ground of

Oglala drunks, who often walk out of the reservation to get their fix and then collapse in abandoned garages or on mattresses by the side of the road. Driving down from Pine Ridge, one often passes these itinerant drinkers heading to White Clay for a toot. The town itself produces a unique garbage of discarded cans and bottles, which pile up in the long grass. Having bought their drink, the Oglala have no place to consume it since under tribal law drinking is forbidden on the reservation. Caught between realms of wet and dry, they down it on the spot, under starry skies.

White Clay has often been called a "death trap," a place of sudden, moody violence where scores are settled within the parameters of intoxication. It was originally a whisky town, and across the West whisky created many such places. The Indians, formed by millennia of total sobriety, were sucked into the vortex of alcohol without warning, disoriented and amazed, seduced and beggared.

The British journalist Andrew Marr, however, makes a slightly different argument in his magisterial survey of the social history of American drink. Marr reasons that the westward expansion of the European settlers broke down their social structures. The frontier, ever unstable and mobile, was a place where disproportionately large numbers of single men found themselves in limbo. Deprived of more reasonable pleasures and comforts—namely, family, women, and children—they took to their bottles. The settlers of the frontier were often Scots-Irish, and they brought with them into this savage no-man's-land their preferred opiate, whisky. But in a frontier economy where money was scarce, they began to use whisky as a bartering item. It became, in effect, a kind of currency. Its introduction to the Indians was neither sinisterly planned nor deliberately "colonial." It was merely an extension of what the whites were doing among themselves.

Whisky, then, was the cutting edge of the white conquest of the Indian lands, but it was not a consciously used tool any more than smallpox was—despite claims to the contrary from certain activists. Whisky was merely the essential element of this male Scots-Irish culture that was expanding westward with very little plan or moral compass. What it unleashed, on both whites and Indians, was unconscious and unpredictable. Drinking on the frontier became its own solace, its own object. It was wild and absurdly extreme on both sides. The popular depiction of swing-door saloons in the West is accurate. There are countless accounts of men drinking for four or five days straight, drinking themselves into oblivion. Whisky was the ideal drug for this desire to self-forget. It was strong, it didn't go bad, and it turned you relatively quickly into a stranger, a madman. It was the first alcohol that North America embraced from coast to coast, the "firewater" that defined its fears and pleasures. The temperance and prohibition movements of later decades were a reaction against the excesses of antisocial whisky drinking.

Prohibition itself, one could argue, was an attempt to repress the lawless psychological states of the frontier, to tame and domesticate and feminize. It made all these problems worse, of course, but its arguments are not entirely different from those of Islam. What the philosopher John Gray has called "the

American war on pleasure" has its roots not just in an ancestral Puritanism but in this secret denial of the inebriated frontier.

But whisky on the private level—in the mind of the nostalgic—does not arouse historical meditations. The scourge of the West is also the golden libation of childhood Christmas, the toddy, the warmer of nights and of long afternoons of sickness, more mysterious to a child, I daresay, than any other drink because it is so repellent and visually attractive at the same time. It is dropped into hot milk—a smoky aftertaste—and into hot water with lemon, stirred with sugar and sipped with a knowledge that the mind is going to be very slightly altered. Thus perhaps whisky was my first drink after all, the first experiencing of mind alteration, of self-distancing. I cannot say if any of my Dionysian uncles were properly speaking a Scotch expert, but it was surely their drink of drinks, their apex elixir. My mother was never far separated from a glass of Famous Grouse and, at Christmas, a special bottle of Black Grouse blended with Islay malts. Whisky is, after all, the only indigenous connoisseur drink that the English-speaking peoples produce, if we skirt politely around the claims of handmade beer. For the Irish and the Scots, it is "ours." It is the drug that is close to the bone, our thread back into the past and its magnificent confusions.

On Islay the best whisky bar in Bowmore is that of the Lochside Hotel, with its long windows overlooking Loch Indaal, its Prawn Marie-Rose served with brown bread, its ale and mushroom Lochside beef pie served with drams of Caol Ila, and its air of deliciously inbred desolation. It is better at night, when the corner bar is filled with toasted old locals chewing their cuds and you can't see the retreated tide. Here is the place to catch up on Jura and older Ardbeg far from the distillery tourists. Here is the place to escape any memory of Bowmore's curious round church and a thing called the MacTaggart Leisure Centre. The drinking is not boisterous or rapid; it is indeed like chewing. The Japanese come with their raincoats and try to talk—through an English-language glass darkly—with the islanders. It is love of Scotch that draws them close, the Japanese afflicted by an affinity of which they are barely conscious. Even they do not seem to know why Japan has become one of the largest whisky producers in the world, and one of the largest consumers of it as well. One of them told me it was "an Asian disease," this love affair with Celtic distillates. Did I know that the first distillery in Japan, the Yamazaki in the outskirts of Kyoto, was positioned to benefit from the world's most beautifully clear water, the same water favored by famed tea master Sen no Rikyu? It is now owned by Suntory. Yes, I was assured, everywhere great whisky is defined by its water! And everywhere the effects of its intoxication were curiously different. The water was different, and so were the drinkers. The Japanese tasters were beady-eyed and loquacious, their lips wet and their heads drooping forward slightly. A slow-motion ecstasy. In myself, Scotch produces a glassy brightness as well, but it is purely internal. The mind goes hard and clear and begins to swim forward with long strokes. Words run ahead of the body. Language flows and ebbs and explodes. The Irish.

. . .

In the East, whisky also possesses a magic charisma. The Emporium mall at Asoke in Bangkok, as I remember, contained on its first floor a glass shrine to Alexander Walker's leather-bound recipe book and an original bottle from the nineteenth century displayed like a relic in a Buddhist shrine. It was exhibited as a talisman, a holy object. The Johnnie Walker myth has grown inexorably in recent years: 130 million bottles a year, sold in virtually every country on earth; that square bottle with its label angled at twenty-four degrees is as instantly recognizable as a Gucci bag or a Subway lunch. The color-coded labels are fetishized from Beirut to Singapore. They are ubiquitous.

Beirut again. One night I was taken to a dinner party at the fifth-floor penthouse of a Sunni construction millionaire. An opulent pad in the Beirut style, fruit bowls and oils and tasseled sofas into which you can sink as if they were deathbeds. The style of Europe, of Paris *banlieues*. Of villas in Saint-Germain-en-Laye and Enghien-les-Bains, of houses on the outskirts of Milan, where the industrial classes get to unpack their lugubrious tastes and their dire sense of material joy. It is quite enjoyable. You have the feeling that no one is going to object to you whipping out a cigar at meal's end. The host was a man of about sixty, and he had a beautiful, sophisticated wife twenty years his junior. They cracked jokes and laughed a lot. They were rich, and they buzzed around the world. It was Thanksgiving, in fact, and they had roasted an enormous turkey with stuffing. Cranberry jelly, gravy, roasted potatoes. The mood was one of wisecracking ease, helped along by a sideboard of alcoholic drinks of which the hosts, being Muslim, did not partake. They were for us, the guests, and the gin and tonics and Kirs were mixed and offered with a charming and unselfconscious civility.

As we waited for dinner, the host gathered his guests around the sofas and said that he had been seeing the most extraordinary ad signs all over Beirut. Had any of us noticed the same ones? They were for a local variety of Red Bull that had just come on the market. Here it was. He whipped out a can from his fridge and showed us. It was called Pussy.

"You thought I was joking? Only in Lebanon. Only in Lebanon would an endurance soft drink be called Pussy. Only here. Imagine that in Egypt? Or in the Gulf? I am seeing signs for Pussy all over town. Everywhere I turn—Pussy. No? They think the locals won't get it?"

"Yes," one of the women cried, "I saw a truck today going up Mount Lebanon—it had the word 'Pussy' on its side. I was wondering—"

"You see? Only in Lebanon. What genius came up with that?" They laughed till they cried.

"Pussy billboards everywhere." The host sighed, leaning back and catching my eye. "You see what kind of people we are. Tremendous."

The tone was therefore worldly and open. After the turkey and the apple pie, completely and authentically American, the bottles arrived. It is not uncommon here in Beirut to see bottles of Blue Label taken out from their special silk-lined cask and made available to guests. Two thousand dollars is a ferocious price for a blended Scotch, but whisky here is a drink of display, a certificate of belonging to a global community of consumers, and its price is a necessary part of its appeal.

I went for arak myself, since I am a single-malt snob, but the aging businessmen around the table claimed that they had heard rumors of a new Johnnie Walker that was becoming available to the superrich, a blend even costlier than Blue Label.

Ah, Johnnie Walker, they muttered appreciatively. Mystery of mysteries, drink of drinks! Even the Muslims who do not drink have opinions about Johnnie Walker. Another guest, a man of about eighty who was also in construction, described the scene on the causeway that connects Saudi Arabia and Bahrain. There is, he said, a halfway house midway across where Saudi drivers returning to their border who are too drunk to drive are sheltered and monitored while they sober up. A remarkable thing, the Saudi appetite for booze, which is famous all over the Middle East. A vile thing, if you think about it. A dark and secretive passion that expressed itself not in gay conviviality and comradely exuberance but in trashed hotel rooms and surly scenes and the halfway house on the causeway, where the drunkards huddled like crack addicts after their debaucheries in Bahrain.

To Muslims living in more tolerant lands, however, the Saudi booze appetite is less shocking than a sign of character related to the overall condition of a people. Everyone knows the Saudis are pigs, the Lebanese often seem to be saying, and that is because they live there and not here. It is because they do not have Pussy in their corner stores, or Johnnie Walker Blue Label. It is because they have not learned how to regulate their desires.

Alcohol is desire, and especially whisky, that supreme but disreputable expression of it.

The host said, "Look at me. I am surrounded by bottles of Johnnie Walker. Am I tempted to join you in a glass? Not at all. I am perfectly happy that you are happy drinking my Johnnie Walker. I don't have any emotions about it whatsoever. It is not about drinking what is forbidden. I have settled in to what I may and may not do. So the issue does not arise. I don't hate Johnnie Walker because he is a symbol of Satan, or you, or the West. We've just eaten turkey with cranberry. Is that a symbol of America? We are not uncomfortable with anything and certainly not with alcohol. It is just not for us. We leave it quietly to one side. Enjoy your Scotch."

East into West

After many years of contemplating the move, and after my mother died, I finally got a little house in Istanbul. It sat on a hill between the northern suburb of Etiler and the old Armenian village of Arnavutköy, with the garish lights of the bridge at Ortaköy visible at night and seabirds wheeling above the cypresses and the stony minaret of the mosque on the side of the valley that swept down to the Bosphorus. My six-month travel turned into a year and then longer. I found myself living in the region I had originally intended merely to visit, and drinking there turned into an experiment of years.

Some places are intended as a withdrawal, a penance. Places where one is doomed to be alone with the self. I moved there during my mother's death, and when I returned after the funeral in England, the *adhan*, the call to prayer, which woke me up every morning at five, did not infuriate me as it might have done otherwise. The enormity of the amplification created by that single speaker tied to the minaret's shaft was enough to penetrate all slumber, to crack all distraction. For a few minutes I was forced to concentrate on the call to prayer, a call to prayer of a religion to which I do not belong. The call would seem to stop on a high note, and I would drift back into grateful sleep; and then, almost enraged, it would recommence, and I would be forced to listen again to the rising and falling tones, the echo of an ancient desert, the hysteria. During those weeks of broken sleep and nightmares, I stopped drinking. It was a way of concentrating on death and its aftermath.

Etiler is one of the more international neighborhoods of Istanbul, affluent and residential, with a bar and restaurant scene stretched along Nispetiye Avenue as it rises toward the hideous Akmerkez Mall. It is not the Istanbul of Sultanahmet restaurant touts armed with battered English, and places where "tribal" women make bread in the window, and the *meyhanes* (or traditional taverns) of Istiklal where you down your raki with plates of *borek* and slowly realize that you are an alien. Etiler, like Levent to the south, is even more Westernized, but it is not a spectacle for Westerners: it's a living facility.

This is what is most known about Turkey, that it is the only Muslim country that is secular, the only one where Muslims can drink legally, even if a mere six percent of Turkish households actually do so. It is famously "Westernized." The founder of the nation, Mustafa Kemal Atatürk, was himself a heavy drinker and was reputed to have died from a surfeit of raki, the Turkish version of arak. It is very likely that he did.

But in recent years the Justice and Development Party, the AKP, of Prime Minister Recep Tayyip Erdoğan—a man who prays devoutly five times a day—has begun to curb its nation's exceptional liberalism in the matter of alcohol. Images of alcohol have been more or less banned from the media, and taxes on it have been raised, so that whereas before a bottle of raki once cost about eight Turkish lira, about five dollars, it now costs thirty-five dollars. The government protests that it is doing nothing to curb Turkish freedoms. It points out that European governments tax alcohol as well, that everywhere it exists governments try to regulate its consumption, its representation. But Erdoğan himself has said that he does not understand why anyone would drink wine with dinner. Why would they drink wine, he has said, "when they can eat the grapes instead?"

In the center of the country, in the conservative heartland, the bars in entire towns are closing down, their licenses discreetly unrenewed. It was difficult to prove empirically, but unlike Beirut, where wine is cosmopolitan and cheap, drinking in Istanbul is expensive and unrefined: French wine, even, is not easy to come by. At even a chic fish place in Bebek, it is going to be Buzbağ, Kavaklidere, a Narince from Central Anatolia, an Öküzgözü, and little else.

Defenders of the government, who probably comprised the majority of the population, argued that there was justification for taxes on alcohol and restrictions on advertising. (Alcohol could no longer be shown in ads for cheese or meze side dishes, foods with which it is traditionally associated.) In the first place, it was popular, and the government would not suffer for being Islamic. Second, alcohol was harmful. Third, it was fun, and the Turkish relationship to fun is complicated.

. . .

Walking through the darkly somber streets of Karaköy or Galata under the song of seagulls, I consider the Brumelia celebrated sixteen hundred years ago under those same seabirds. It was Christianity, not Islam, that banned it, but the present religion in any case would not have suffered it for a moment. Constantinople was made orderly, as befitted a metropolis that first made monotheism a state religion. When you walk up toward Cihangir from Selim III's brick armory, the Tophane, and look back over the city, what you see is a skyline of monotheistic certainty, its minarets once compared by a visiting Herman Melville to the slim, funereal forms of graveyard cypresses.

There would be no global Christianity without this city, which later, under the Ottomans, came to be known as the Abode of Happiness. Constantinople is where the pagan world ended, and where Dionysus met his untimely demise. Its stony melancholy is imperial, austere, and attuned to the one god, whether that of Justinian or that of Mehmet the Conqueror. "Gong-tormented" and vaporous, as Patrick Leigh Fermor famously described it in *Mani,* that exquisite meditation on, among many other things, the long-drawn-out and misunderstood genius of Byzantium.

It is not only the stones that make the city feel so weighted; there is also a folk memory so deep that it will never emerge again into consciousness. The celebrants of Brumelia, the Greeks, did not disappear. They merged into the city's bloodstream.

To those who live here, Istanbul's slightly overheated trendiness does not obscure this essential fact. It's an intricate city, difficult to know, labyrinthine and secretive and withdrawn. Its rarefied sadness is what is charismatic about it. Accordingly, the heavy drinking of raki is not joyous; it is brooding, internalized. But raki also heals.

When looking for a bar, I bear in mind Buñuel's injunctions, even in Istanbul. But here one is thrown back eventually on the Pera Palace Hotel, whose famous bar has undergone a revolting and purposeless renovation. No matter. It is still Agatha Christie's bar, and one cannot ask for much more than that.

It was here in the Pera, as every tourist knows, that she wrote *Murder on the Orient Express.* Istanbul was where she liked to work, where she perhaps liked to escape her philandering husband. On this occasion a chocolate model of the Eiffel Tower stands in the salon that separates the lobby from the ballroom. Here all is Ottoman-style domes and columns and carpets, a perfect fabricated Eastern set piece. A great mother-of-pearl cabinet dominates the far end, inside which vellum books lie on their sides. (Has someone just been reading them?) The Orient Bar, newly tarted up, adjoins these orientalist rooms and, with its framed oils of tenebrous sultans, partakes of their mood and invites one to sit at the heavy counter and drink a house cocktail, the Martian.

I like to walk around the Pera anyway, a tomb of nineteenth-century hotel technology and traveler frivolity. On the walls by the elevator, I love the paintings by minor Frenchmen showing girls in European parks covered with doves and pigeons, or views of the Asian Bosphorus when it was still an idyllic and somewhat medieval place, with kiosks and bearded men in turbans lounging under mulberry trees. The old Istanbul that was expeditiously buried under freeway cement around the year 1960.

The iron scrollwork of the 1890 elevator soars up to unknown pleasures of upper floors, and the stairs are soundless with the pile carpet. But this is just, for me, the appendix to the Orient Bar, which in winter is empty but that beckons night after night, and not only because of its sureness of touch with staple mixes. It's a bar that meets all the Buñuelian requirements: no music, no youth, no men in beards, no strange lighting. Though I might add that it seems a shame that one of the wall-mounted sultans is not the infamous IV, who died of alcohol poisoning after countless drinking parties. During which, chroniclers assure us, he would shoot arrows at passersby from a window of the Topkapi Palace, or run disguised into the streets and kill random individuals with a sword, by way of inebriated amusement. The Dionysian folly of alcohol was running rampant, to point out an obvious paradox, in the veins of the Islamic world's most powerful leader.

Indeed, I thought quite often of Murad IV as I sat alone at the Orient Bar that winter, for he was without question one of the most amazing of Ottoman personalities. Drinking here, how could one not?

Born in 1612 he ascended the throne in 1623 and died drunk at twenty-eight. During a revolt of the Janissaries in 1632, he purged the army and executed twenty thousand rebels in Anatolia. Then he successfully invaded Persia. He also banned coffee and alcohol throughout the empire. (The ban on coffee did not last, despite that substance's obviously "intoxicating" effects.)

The man who banned alcohol, however, became its greatest addict. The historian of Istanbul, John Freely, says this about the affliction of Murad's later years:

> During the latter years of his reign Murad became addicted to drink, apparently under the influence of an alcoholic layabout known as Bekri ("the Drunkard") Mustafa. The story of Murad's meeting with Bekri Mustafa is told by the historian Demetrius Cantemir. It seems that Murad was walking through the market quarter in disguise one day when he came across Bekri Mustafa "wallowing in the dirt dead drunk." Murad was intrigued by the drunkard and brought him back to the palace, where Mustafa introduced the sultan to the joys of wine, showing him that the best cure for a hangover is more of the same. Bekri Mustafa soon died of drink, leaving Murad bereft, as Cantemir writes:
>
> > *At his death the emperor order'd the whole Court to go into mourning, but caus'd his body to be buried with great pomp in a tavern among the hogsheads. After his decease the emperor declar'd he never enjoy'd one merry day, and whenever Mustapha chanc'd to be mentioned, was often seen to burst out into tears, and to sigh from the bottom of his heart.*

This didn't stop him from turning into a homicidal maniac. Dying of cirrhosis of the liver in 1640, he was buried in the *turbe* of the Blue Mosque. His younger brother Ibrahim inherited the throne and became a sex maniac who, before being deposed by the Janissaries and then strangled, had become known to the populace as Ibrahim the Mad. Interestingly and perhaps unsurprisingly, he invaded, and subdued, Crete in order to finance his unaffordable debaucheries.

The sultans were not just the leaders of the Ottoman state.

They were also caliphs, Islam's spiritual leaders, descended in one way or another from the Prophet. Murad IV was perhaps the first caliph to die of alcoholism, but he was certainly not the last.

In the eighteenth and nineteenth centuries, as the Ottomans became more exposed to Europeans and began to lose battles and wars to them, the sultans came more and more under the sway of alcoholic tastes, in much the same way that they came under the sway of rococo architecture. Murad V, for example, who ascended the throne in 1876, had accompanied his uncle Sultan Abdülaziz on a tour of Europe in 1867, where he had acquired a ferocious and, for his advisers, regrettable appetite for champagne and cognac. His alcoholism was so severe that he was unable to go through with the coronation ceremony, during which a new sultan was girded with the sword of the dynastic founder Osman.

Murad was deposed a few months later and died of diabetes in 1904, a caliph of Islam so habitually intoxicated that he could not function either in the service of the state or as the head of a religion that prohibits alcohol.

Thus I thought as I drank the Martian house cocktail at the Orient, a green mix of some kind that is offered free to clients who look as if they might spend a fair amount. An order of two aged Old Havana rums usually qualified me, and so I could sit at that long bar alone at 6:10 sharp with dark rums and imagine Efendim Christie seated at the far end with her toddy and notebook. On those days, however, when I could not face the long cab ride to a bar in the city, not even the Orient, I walked down from my street on the edges of Etiler to Bebek, passing above the sweep of the Bosphorus close to the point where Xerxes threw over his pontoon bridge during the invasion of Hellas in 480 B.C. The Valide Pasha Palace now sits on that waterfront, and north of it socialite fish restaurants and nightclubs, among which stands the Bebek Hotel with a bar facing out over the water to the gold-lit palaces and the baroque gardens on the far side.

To the Otel Bebek, as it is known in Turkish, I come at night, hesitant and alone but enjoying the walk down through wooded hills, along winding roads of cottages and pine trees where the stray dogs sometimes snarl and follow like hyenas. There are times when I have to save myself with stones. (And didn't Byron also complain in his letters of the ravenous dog packs of Istanbul?) It is the preamble to a gin and tonic on the deck under the gas heaters. Yet at the same time, I notice a bottle of Famous Grouse standing on one of the glass shelves behind the bar, as it would never do in a bar of comparable stylishness in a Western country.

I take to ordering it every night before the gin and tonic as a memory of some kind, though I have never drunk it before. With Mama's tipple in hand, I walk out onto the deck alone. There is never anyone here in winter, understandably. I stand over the floodlit waters where hundred of seagulls sit above a glittering watery stratum of hovering jellyfish. In the pale green depths, swarms of silver fish can also be seen darting underneath the jellyfish, picked out by the lights. The lights of Asia rise up on the far side, a huge Turkish flag illumined in the distance, and between us and them the silhouettes of great ships pass in the night on their way to Odessa.

It is here that I come face to face with the incompleteness of what I know about my mother. She returns to me with that cheap smoky whisky pooling on the tongue and the sight of the brilliantly lit gulls sitting in a silent swarm on the waters. During her last night, I sat with her at the Royal Sussex in Brighton during a sinister storm while my niece slept on the floor. By then she was already unconscious on morphine, and her hand pulsed with reactions arising in an unconscious mind that might well have known that it was dying. I had known very little about the circumstances of a suddenly lethal disease—doctors call pancreatic cancer "the silent killer"—which had only been diagnosed four days earlier. A death swift and merciful in some ways, but mysterious for that same reason. There had been no time for farewells, and there was a chance that she would not have wanted a farewell anyway. She had a brusque contempt for sentimentality, like all deeply sentimental people.

The shame of it was that I had not been able to share with her a last Famous Grouse, and instead, therefore, I have to drink it by myself in a bar in Istanbul, in the ghostly setting of the Otel Bebek, with its bow-tied barmen and chintz armchairs, with a curious glass bowl of limes on the bar.

The Bosphorus was a place she loved, probably because Lord Byron had swum across it and because Byron, too, loved it, as quite bad passages of *Don Juan* attest. It was my mother, in fact, who called my attention to the fact that these waters were "very

English" insofar as they had inspired many of our countrymen and countrywomen. It was their Hellenism, in one way; but it was also the Ottoman sense of ease and, perhaps, their fine-mannered late imperial sadness mitigated, in the Tulip Era, by full-moon parties lit by wandering tortoises bearing candles.

The Istanbul-loving wife of the British ambassador to the court of Ahmed III, Lady Mary Montagu, has left us superlative letters, which Byron did not hesitate to recall:

> The European with the Asian shore,
> Sprinkled with palaces, the ocean stream
> Here and there studded with a seventy-four,
> Sophia's cupola with golden gleam;
> The cypress groves; Olympus high and hoar;
> The twelve isles, and the more than I could dream,
> Far less describe, present the very view
> Which charm'd the charming Mary Montagu.

My mother loved the city because the sea runs through it, and everywhere the seagulls turn in vast spirals. She lived, less spectacularly, in Hove for the same reason. Istanbul adopted her ghost, or it could have been the other way round, because one would never know. The Turks assure me this was normal. Dead mothers naturally look in to see if their children are all right.

There is a well-known place to drink raki by the Bosphorus underneath the castle built by Mehmed II when he cut off the grain supply to Constantinople in 1453, the Rumeli Hisari. It's called the Rumeli Balikcisi, and at night you can sit on a terrace overlooking the road and look up at the soaring bridge to Asia, lit up in charmingly absurd lollipop colors. It's a place to explore the subtly different types of raki.

There is Yeni Raki—"new raki"—which unlike traditional raki, fermented from grape pomace, is derived from beets. Like all other aniseed-flavored drinks—ouzo, pastis, arak, and absinthe—it can then be drunk either neat (which the Turks, adopting the French word, call *sek*) or with chilled water added. The water, of course, induces spontaneous emulsification, the so-called "louche" effect: absinthe turns cloudy when water is dripped into it through a cube of sugar, thus obscuring its lovely green color. *La fée verte,* absinthe was always called—"the green fairy."

When drinking raki, I cannot help but recall the admirable slotted spoons that are used for the preparation of absinthe, the sugar cube resting upon the holes through which ice-cold water will pass. Raki is not prepared this way, but it is also an aniseed fermentation that possesses a colossal alcohol content, and it enjoys in Turkey the same universality that absinthe enjoyed in France at the end of the nineteenth century. Curiously, raki only became popular at that very same time. It was a product of the liberalization of Ottoman society in a century dominated by a collective imitation of Europe. It is a sister drink to absinthe, a creation of the same period.

But whereas absinthe was banned in the West by 1915, condemned as a psychoactive drug containing the supposedly dangerous chemical thujone, raki became the national drink of the first secular Islamic nation. The differences between them, as regards addiction, psychoactive properties, and potency, are pretty much nil.

Absinthe gained popularity first in the French Army, where it was used—much like tonic water and its quinine—as an antimalarial. Its demonic reputation at the end of the century is hard to explain. But a drink that has an alcohol level of anywhere between 50 and 75 percent cannot fail to disequilibrize the drinker. Raki usually comes in at a slightly lower 45 percent, but that is enough to expose the galloping imbiber to a bout of what will feel like dementia.

Public displays of drunkenness are unusual in Turkey. Sometimes, as you are walking nocturnally along a street near a commercial area like Taksim, or a tougher joint like Tarlabaşi, a man in the grip of that madness will brush against you. But in the majority of cases you will be struck by how tragic, by how isolated and silent he will seem, how frozen by social restriction, how inoffensive in his lack of freedom. He is not the wild drunk on a street in London who will happily take a swing at you. The violence is there, but it seems more contained, more frigid. In any case, the terrace of the Balıkçisi will never offer such an experience because here the drinking of fine raki is studious and contemplative, attuned at all times to the demands of a mild connoisseurship.

Here I add the water because I prefer it to the *sek* style. I relish the way that, as soon as the water has been added, the waiter will come up with a pair of tongs and delicately drop a single cube of ice into my glass. Thus chilled and clouded, my Yeni is ready for daydreaming.

I wonder, as I drop in the ice cubes myself, at the rakis mentioned around 1630 by Evliya Çelebi, the Ottoman travel writer who left a great and beautifully irrational book called the *Seyahatname*, which describes both the Asian provinces of the Ottoman Empire and, in rather more detail, the city of Constantinople itself, of which he was a native—and one often forgets that under the Ottomans the city was never officially called Istanbul.

Çelebi, who was an indignant and overprotesting teetotaler, enumerated banana rakis, the cinnamon and clove rakis sold all over Istanbul in defiance of the Islamic assumption that even one drop of it (as Çelebi himself put it) was sinful. At that time, there were a hundred distilleries in the city, a fantastical production implying an equally fantastical consumption.

Here is an aghast Çelebi on the alcoholism of Galata, the European quarter on the far side of the Golden Horn, largely inhabited by Italians:

In Galata there are two hundred taverns and wine-shops where the Infidels divert themselves with music and drinking. The taverns are celebrated for the wines of Ancona, Mudanya, Smyrna and Tenedos. The word *gunaha* (temptation) is most particularly to be applied to the taverns of Galata because there all kinds of playing and dancing boys, mimics and fools flock together and delight themselves, day and night. When I passed through this district I saw many bareheaded and bare-footed lying drunk in the street; some confessed aloud the state they were in by singing such couplets as these: "I drank the ruby wine, how drunk, how drunk am I! / A prisoner of the locks, how mad, how mad am I!" Another sang, "My foot goes to the tavern, nowhere else. / My hand grasps tight the cup and nothing else. Cut short your sermon for no ears have I / But for the bottle's murmur, nothing else."

Çelebi protests many times that he is merely recording these strange phenomena for the benefit of his friends. But it should be remembered that he was a page and a favorite of Murad IV, hired by the sultan because he was reportedly able to recite the entirety of the Koran in seven hours. His acquaintance with alcohol might not have been what he pretended. The visions and flights of fancy that punctuate his book suggest some kind of intoxication was at work—in one famous passage he recalls seeing the Prophet in a dream, and duly records that his hands were "boneless" and smelled of roses. It could have been a night's dabbling with cinnamon raki.

By now I could faintly distinguish between the different styles of raki, but not to a degree that would ever constitute discernment. It felt more melancholic, more grave, than arak—who knows why? More like absinthe, lacking only the more elaborate ritual of the "green fairy."

But undeniably the upper-end rakis possess perfumes that linger in the lungs. They make you want to sit and sink into a mellow and mildly useless despondency, to mimic the sudden cloudiness in the glass. It is the perfect drink for introspection and observation. "What a lovely drink this is," Atatürk once said of it, with a touch of regret, "it makes one want to be a poet." It did not make him into one.

Wherever one is, one is susceptible to the addictions that are on offer. In the rituals of day by day and night by night, one chooses the opiate that is least inauthentic to that place.

One night at the bottom of my little street, Samyeli Sokak, a new sign appeared at the corner of the connecting road, a bright blue sign for Efes beer that announced the opening of that most miraculous thing, a *liquor store*.

There was a new window filled with curious bottles, the most obvious of which was Olmeca tequila and brands of gin I had never heard of. It seemed to be run by a young husband-and-wife team who called out "*merhaba*" every time I walked by, obviously hopeful that this interloping foreigner might be exactly the kind of neighborhood customer they were intending to hit up. Not only that, but the store was open *all night long*. A twenty-four-hour vodka and tequila depot right on my doorstep, but one that was never filled with customers that I could see. It was like a friendly porn store open all night to those who knew how to shop with discretion.

But every night, as I struggled up the steep hill, as often as not fairly inebriated after an evening of raki by the water, I passed the lit window with the woman sitting there alone eating potato chips and our eyes met for a moment. "Come in," hers said, fully aware of the temptations of those displays of Olmeca tequila. "Better not," mine replied as I walked on, but glad that a bottle of Olmeca was now on hand. "You have no idea where that will lead me."

There is, however, one more side to the hidden life of Istanbul that the drinker, the believer in wine, cannot ignore. Underlying the official Islam of the Turks and the Ottoman state, there has always been the near heresy of Sufism and the sects that are sometimes grouped, perhaps erroneously, under that name. Sufism is not a Turkish invention—it seems to have reached its greatest blossoming in Persia. Rumi and Hāfez, its two greatest poets, spoke Persian by birth, though Rumi was born in what is today Afghanistan.

But Rumi's family was forced west by the Mongol invasions, and they eventually settled in Konya, in the Seljuk Turk sultanate of Rum. As Hāfez is the poet of Shiraz, so Rumi is the poet of Konya. It was there that he held high academic office before meeting the incandescent Shams e-Tabriz, the wandering dervish or mendicant who changed his life.

Konya is one of the holiest cities of modern Turkey, and Turks therefore claim Rumi as their own. The Mevlevi school of "whirling" dervishes was founded by Rumi in Konya, and its ritual, the *sema*, has become the country's preeminent tourist spectacle.

The Sufis relished wine as the supreme metaphor of love. Their poems are time and again celebrations of drunkenness, taverns, wine cups, intoxicated madness, all intended metaphorically but described as if physically known.

Rumi writes:

Come, come, awaken all true drunkards!
Pour the wine that is Life itself
O cupbearer of the Eternal Wine,
Draw it now from Eternity's Jar.
This wine doesn't run down the throat
But it looses torrents of words.

In Sufi metaphors, wine is the love that inebriates the soul; the wine cup is the body. The *saaqi* or cupbearer is an aspect of God's grace. The lingering effect of love is called a "hangover."

Many a miniature depicts Hāfez tipsy in the wine bars of Kharabat, the tavern district of Shiraz, being served by voluptuous cupbearers. There is no memory of such a district in the Shiraz of today. Moreover, in Shia Sufic poetry, the hidden imam is sometimes called the *Pir-e Kharabat,* the Elder of the Kharabat or the Great Drunkard.

Hāfez writes:

Cupbearer, it is morning, fill my cup with wine.
Make haste, the heavenly sphere knows no delay.
Before this transient world is ruined and destroyed,
Ruin me with a beaker of rose-tinted wine.
The sun of the wine dawns in the east of the goblet.
Pursue life's pleasure, abandon dreams,
And the day when the wheel makes pitchers of my clay,
Take care to fill my skull with wine!
We are not men for piety, penance and preaching
But rather give us a sermon in praise of a cup of clear wine.
Wine-worship is a noble task, O Hafiz;
Rise and advance firmly to your noble task.

One night my friend Sébastien de Courtois, a French scholar of Islam, took me to the Nurettin Cerrahi Tekkesi, a little-known dervish school of the seventeenth-century saint Cerrahi Halveti, whose shrine lies in the back streets of the poor and deeply religious neighborhood of Karagunduz near the Fatih Mosque. Fatih, or this part of it, is now one of the most religiously conservative areas of Istanbul. The Islamic revival is welling up quietly in places like Karagunduz.

We walked there through heavy snow, past textile shops and steamed-up cafés, asking the way from the fruit stands as we went. The *tekke* stood on a dark side street, and in front of it burly beggar women in black held out their hands to the worshippers coming into the gate. Beyond the gate there was a long passage, barred windows through which we peered into the saint's sanctuary and burial shrine, the floors covered with dark red carpets. In the small lobby the sexes separated and took off their shoes. The women went up a stone staircase to a screened gallery that overlooked the main prayer room.

Sébastien took me through the first of the prayer rooms. It was crowded on a Thursday night, the men all in white skullcaps, listening to a recitation in the Arabic of the Koran relayed through the adjoining rooms by small speakers. The walls were covered with gilded framed Koranic verses, with the slightly crazed faces of former leaders caught by ancient cameras long ago. The men began to kneel and incline forward in prayer. Sébastien and I moved into other rooms until we were in a kind of salon next to the main prayer room. Into this heavily embellished salon the practitioners were flowing as they tried to press their way into the room beyond. An imam read there before a wall of dark blue Iznik tiles, amid lamps fringed with green glass beads.

The room filled with men, locals in jeans and work shirts,

their heads in white caps. On these walls there were racks of ancient flutes, framed calligraphy, old paintings of Constantinople, shelves with a ceramic decorative scimitar, and a glass cube with Koranic quotations. The men began to form lines, but others sat on the little sofas against the walls. In the main room, the recitations had ended and a chanting had begun—a slow repetition of what sounded like the words *"allahallah."*

As all the men repeated it, they slowly turned their heads to the left and then to the right, dipping their foreheads down on the beat and the first syllable of the word *allah.*

This chant quickened until the heads were rolling left and right, the eyes closed, with a loud exhalation of breath at the end of each phrase. It was like the sudden utterance of a war band. We got up and walked to the open doors giving into the shrine.

A series of circles had formed, the men holding hands. They turned slowly clockwise, their heads still turning to left and right, dipping, the bodies bending slightly to the right as they uttered the same words. In the salon, the old men seated on the sofas made the same motions with their heads, their eyes closed. They were inducted into the same trance. The *sema*, the ceremony. Drummers had appeared, in white turbans. At the center of the circle stood a single dervish in his tall camel-hair *sikke* hat symbolizing the tombstone of his ego. He was younger than the leaders conducting the chants, the mustache carefully trimmed.

The chanting ebbed and flowed, changed rhythm and speed. The men began to sweat and half-dance as they turned. Something had clicked between them, and they were now fused into a single whole. The man in the *sikke* began to rotate in the center of the space. His arms wide, dressed in white, he spun like a sycamore seed falling: an expression of pure intoxication.

It was, in some way, pre-Islamic. A hunting band dancing on a mountain before or after a kill. A war band in its trance. The old women above rocked their heads in time to the drums. This had nothing in common with the sweet and prettified Whirling Dervish spectacles that tourists enjoy all over the city in summer. This was like a sweat lodge.

The leader led the inmost circle, his body lunging left and right as he danced sideways hand in hand with his neighbors. The whirler's head inclined to the right as he turned. His body had gone limp. It looked as if he were unconscious on his feet, his mind wandering into the "other world."

"The ceremony," Sébastien was whispering, "was invented by Rumi himself. It has come down to us like this—and to think these are locals who have learned it in their spare time. Twenty years ago this would have been outlawed." Atatürk had banned the lodges, and they had revived only the last ten years.

I went back to the sofa at the back of the room and wedged myself between two groaning, head-rocking gentlemen in their later years. I slumped against the wall and felt my head spin. I steadied myself with both hands and looked through the window in the wall and up at the women's gallery, where I could see the rocking heads of the old women behind the screen. A few younger boys came in late and knelt on the carpet and bowed their heads down to it. They looked over at me with a slight confusion, then rose to join the collective meditation.

Sébastien walked over and sat at the neighboring table. "You look pale. Are you all right?"

"I just got a little light-headed. It happens."

"It's a strange experience, I know. The first time especially."

I feel drunk, I thought, *as drunk as they are.*

The dance went on, and it occurred to us that after two hours, it might be opportune to make a quiet exit.

But before we could agree, the ceremony itself began to wind down, and the men who had crammed the shrine room began to pour back out into the salon. As they did so, they parted to create a narrow passage, and it was clear that down this gap the leader would walk, destined to park himself in a red velvet arm-chair that was hastily being prepared for him next to the sofa where they were seated. It happened in the blink of an eye. The leader, mopping his brow, came down toward them, surrounded by awestruck followers.

He seated himself with a sigh in the armchair, and two helpers came behind him. They pulled open his shirt and placed inside it a length of padding to shield his skin from the sweat-soaked fabric. His white cap was also replaced. He was about sixty, with cunning eyes and a short gray beard, cropped iron hair. He said, *"Cigari,"* and a man lunged forward immediately with a Camel Wide. Another sprang forward to provide the lighter flame. As the acolytes swarmed around their leader, we were trapped. We got up to leave at once. The leader blew out a lazy plume of smoke, cast an eye upon us, and said in Turkish, "You don't have to leave." We had no choice but to sit down again and endure the entire audience. The leader was going to take questions from his disciples about life, death, and all things in between. In doing this, he would go through about eight cigarettes.

As he began answering the questions of his disciples—they sighed together and placed their hands on their hearts every time he said something profound—a Pakistani journalist appeared at his side with a Turkish interpreter, one of the disciples. The man had a formidable gray beard and grinned at everything the leader said, though it was obvious he spoke not a word of Turkish. He asked some simple-minded questions in English, and the leader replied with a verse in Koranic Arabic.

"Understand?" he asked the Pakistani in English.

No, the man did not get the Arabic.

"The leader says that by dancing this way, we pass over into the other world. We shed our ego in this life."

"Yes, shed the ego," the Pakistani repeated.

"We shed our normal consciousness."

"Ah yes." The Pakistani suddenly looked tense and a little at sea. "You mean we pass into a different state of mind?"

"It's as Rumi says. We drink the wine of love."

"Ah yes, love."

"Love is what we are striving for. It is all about love. And no one can make love grow by itself. It cannot be forced. It must come of its own accord."

There was a slight tension now. It was the idea of wine, even metaphorical wine. One can see why fundamentalists have always hated Sufism. For not only did Sufis use wine as a metaphor of intoxicating love, they also advocated love of Christians and Jews.

The advantage of the Pakistani's presence was that now I could understand some of the exchanges better. The leader chatted and cajoled, chain-smoking furiously, cracking little jokes and demanding some chocolate biscuits and tea that boys were carrying around the room on precariously balanced trays. It lasted an hour. Eventually, the leader tired of it and called an end to the questions. All rose. There was an orderly and polite scramble for the doors. We put on our shoes outside, under dripping icicles, and came back into the street, mobbed by the burly beggars in black.

On the far side of Fevzi Paşa, the streets slope downward through ancient neighborhoods now rebuilt as cement tenements, their surfaces barnacled with satellite dishes. The lamps strung high up between them rock back and forth in the winds, making the alleys flash in and out of darkness. I went down alone, having said my fond goodnights to Monsieur de Courtois, and the mood of Sufi intoxication persisted until I came to the oval plaza of dark orange buildings where a forbidding Roman column stands, the Column of Marcian.

In the middle of the neighborhood whose tradesmen like to dervish, this gray granite column stands marooned supporting a Corinthian capital and a square block of eroded marble. It was erected by the praetor of the emperor Marcian in A.D. 455. The pedestal has four sides bearing a sculpture of a winged Nike, a cryptogram of Christ, and a symbolic fish. The slots of the Latin letters, which were once filled with bronze, are empty but they can be read: "Look upon this statue and column erected for the Emperor Marcian by his praetor Tatianus." The Turks call this column the Kiz Taşi, the "column of the girls," because of the delicate carved Nike with her flowing robes and her outlines of long disappeared wings. I thought in that moment of the carved relief of the bacchic dancing girl I had seen at the Temple of Dionysus in Baalbek. It was the same motion, a girl moving forward as if dancing: a reminder that in that world it was also the girls who danced drunk and who were immortalized accordingly, whose volatile and ecstatic forms were celebrated as if they would last forever.

Twilight at the Windsor Hotel

At 6:10 sharp I come down from my decrepit room at the Windsor Hotel in Cairo, down the freezing stairs wound around an elevator shaft of such perilous ancientness that the heart does a little two-step at the thought of actually getting into the elevator itself. Nevertheless Mustafa is there waiting with the filthy iron doors held open for me, a ghost in a dark blue uniform that has probably been worn by generations of elevator boys since the days when the Windsor was the British Officers' Mess in Cairo. His yellow eyes light up expecting a tip. "Sir?" he cries, raising a hand to invite me into his little carpeted cage. It is his duty, after all, to carry drunkards up and down from their tawdry rooms to the famous bar on the second floor, and no matter if they are afraid for their lives; he must carry them.

He does this by means of a manual brass switch. "How punctual you are, *habibi*," his eyes say as I walk past him refusing. (The hand-operated car is surely a death trap, though I will likely need it later.) I come down to the bar, and as usual in these days of trouble and strife in Egypt, it is empty. The never-extinguished TV, however, continues to bravely relay a stream of belly-dance shows to synthesizer music. The barrel chairs look sinisterly inviting. But one cannot forget that Tahrir Square is only a short walk away. The streets are filled with a strange, seething anxiety and self-hatred. This winter the tourists have stayed home or ventured to the Seychelles instead.

An ancient and venerable bar must have a barman exuding those same qualities. The Windsor has Marco. Marco is about five foot four but musters the firmest and most intimate of male handshakes. You immediately wonder whether it might be possible that a very young Marco once pulled pints for Lawrence Durrell back in the day. Cairo is a city where nothing, but nothing, is forgotten. The walls of the stairwell, for example, are darkly rich with travel posters—hand-painted, one would say—issued from the offices of Swissair in the 1920s. The scenes are of cobbled squares in Germany long obliterated by the Royal Air Force. Of Saint Moritz filled with Weimar-era millionaires. The hotel was originally built as a bathhouse for the royal family around 1900. It then became an annex of the famous Shepheard's Hotel, which was burned down by a mob during the Revolution of 1952.

The Windsor is my favorite bar in the Middle East. It is, when you first enter it, still an officers' mess equipped with all the expected decorations of a male space: dozens of large and small antlers protrude from its walls, some so small they are like the bones of tiny extinct species unique to the Sahara. The chandeliers are rings of enmeshed antlers. Antelopes, gazelles, ibex, dark wood, low bookcases, shaded lamps, and bar shelves filled with dusty bottles of Omar Khayyam wine and Stella, the Egyptian national beer. It is a perfect anachronism. It must have been one of the bars of Fermor and Durrell in 1942.

It was here that Lawrence of Arabia stormed into the bar after taking Aqaba and returning in triumph to Cairo, a scene famously re-created by David Lean in a grander setting probably inspired by Shepheard's, which lay two blocks away at the edge of the Ezbekia park and which has now been replaced by a miserable gas station.

Lawrence at the Windsor bar in 1917, scandalously dressed as a Bedu and demanding a drink: what other bar would you want to drink at?

The Windsor sits unnoticed within the backstreets of Cairo's downtown, the core of the nineteenth-century city that has for decades decayed like compost until it is almost unrecognizable as the downtown that was once magnificent, the city of King Farouk and Omar Sharif and Om Kalthoum. A city of Parisian boulevards and balconied apartment blocks lifted from the Rue Réaumur. The city of the Café Riche and wondrous hotel bars and a life of flaneurs rarely inconvenienced by religion. The Paris of the East, *pace* Beirut.

I order a gin and tonic, but alas there is no tonic. There is no explanation for this dire lacuna. Instead there is soda, so I can have a whisky soda and a plate of slippery yellow thermos beans. I notice then, as I sit there with three or four Egyptian gentlemen of the elderly and bohemian variety (the two things now being virtually synonymous), that Egyptian cell phones sometimes erupt with a tune I know well but that takes some time to pin down—it is, quite unbelievably, Vaughan Williams's "The Lark Ascending." How has this fragment of English classical music found its way into the repertory of the contemporary Egyptian cell phone? There is no one to ask, since no one knows what it is.

Looking over now, I see that these gentlemen are of the vaguely literary kind. Suave Egyptian men now in their seventies who wear those enormous sunglasses that are perfectly oval, with pale safari suits and pocket squares. The noses blunt and squat, the skin heavily scarred and blotched, the manners exquisite. Men of another era, the era of Sadat, I suppose, and by legacy of the golden 1960s, when this part of Cairo was a paradise of conversation and erotic dalliance. One of them comes over to the bar on unsteady legs to order another shot of Biulli's Egyptian whisky. It's a pretty raw drink, but what is familiar soothes.

"British?" he says, shaking my hand for some reason. The eyes are quite beautifully mad behind the tinted ovals of glass, and he leans toward me as Egyptian men sometimes do, suddenly a little too intimate but nevertheless unconcerned by one's stiff-necked reactions. He whispers heavily in my ear: "Tallyho!"

The British left their mark on this city, on this faded and rotting downtown. They left their bars, for one thing. They left a memory that has taken decades to fade out, of a hard-drinking military elite that mostly despised the place to which it had been posted. But then they were the last wave of the Europeans who washed over Egypt beginning with Napoléon's invasion of 1798. That so-called Army of Scholars, among other things, ushered in a revival of Egyptian liquor. But it eventually led to the aforementioned boulevards and to the incredible buildings of downtown Cairo and Alexandria. It led to the creation of a unique city now famous, if it is famous at all, through the works (if we exempt the incomparable Naguib Mahfouz) of the novelist Alaa Al Aswany. And in particular *The Yacoubian Building*.

In his foreword to the English version of that book, Aswany—who was originally a dentist—describes going with a real estate agent around downtown looking for a place to house a new dental clinic. To him, a middle-class Egyptian, this decaying core of the city was unknown, a revelation:

This experience did, however, bring me an important thought: what was the secret of the significance of Downtown? Why wasn't Downtown just like the other districts of Cairo? In fact, Downtown is not just a residential or commercial center; it is a lot more than that. It represents a whole epoch, an epoch during which Egypt was characterized by tolerance and an amazing capacity to absorb people of different nationalities, cultures, and religions. Muslims, Christians, and Jews, Armenians, Greeks, and Italians—all of them lived in Egypt for long centuries and considered it their true home. Downtown was tantamount to an embodiment of Egypt's great capacity to absorb different cultures and melt them in a single human crucible. Downtown was also, in my opinion, an example of Egypt's project of modernization, which extended from the Muhammad Ali years up to the death of Gamal Abdel Nasser in 1970. It was inevitable that Downtown should wither away thereafter, its importance declining with the ending of the qualities that it represented. The culture of co-existence came to an end and, beginning with the eighties, Egypt fell into the grip of Wahhabite-Salafite thinking, in the face of which Egypt's open, moderate reading of Islam retreated.

I go out into the streets that form a warren between Al-Alfi
Bey and 26th July, streets of somnolent trees that look like fossils
of ancient forests, of the cafés that are spread out under white
strip lights with rows of *shish* pipes and their baskets of coals
smoking in the cold. Al-Alfi leads toward the Midan Orabi, an
open space around which the *shish* cafés are scattered in carless
alleys that also sustain a few last *baladi* or local bars. The gaudi-
est is Scheherazade, which lies at the top of a flight of ominous
steps whose walls are covered with the peeling pictures of belly
dancers of yore.

The club is a single room with a stage at the far end and a
decor of yearning Arabian nightmares. I sometimes come here
and drink my Stellas and watch the tubby girls having their
bras filled with pound notes—paltry sums compared to what
you would see in a belly dancer's bra in Beirut or Dubai. There
is now a slightly harassed, furtive atmosphere in these sorts
of places, as if the slutty girls hired by management to induce
heavy consumption in their guests can never quite forget that
out in the streets all the girls are now in headscarves. Their un-
covered, inviting hair is now more than ever an anomaly. A sign
that inside the Scheherazade they are fair game.

Nearby, on the far side of 26th July—and even off the high-
wattage sidewalks of Talaat Harb, where thousands of manne-
quins stand in windows displaying modest fashions for newly
modest women—there are other, even more discreet *baladi* and
belly-dance joints that have now withdrawn their more obvious
signs and that exist inside a consensual secrecy.

On 26th July, among the clothes stores, there is a tiny alley
named after the Scarabee Hotel, which stands at its entrance.

The Scarabee Alley leads past yet more fashion stores, past the down-at-heel lobby of the hotel, past cafés built into walls where the backgammon games are always at fever pitch.

I come here when I want a *shish* in the courtyard cafés that lie at the end of the alley, in spaces that are squeezed between the vertical grandeur of old apartment blocks. The Scarabee Alley is a secret place that has not yet been gutted and sanitized, but its days are surely numbered.

Even deeper into its bowels there lies a cluster of girlie bars: to the left, the LaVie Hotel and a club at ground level, and to the right the Meame and the Miscellany, which advertise themselves on a horizontal sign above the passageway that leads to them: *Casino and Theater Miscellany.* At dusk, as the small mosques all around—and a dozen televisions and radios—break into the muezzin's song, the lights are switched on by the café owners, and the passageway leading to the clubs comes alive with groomed hustlers and tall, swaying girls in lace-up heeled leather boots.

I have often seen the scarfed matrons puffing at their pipes in the courtyard café watch these creatures arrive with expressions of wide-eyed horror, which at the same time accommodates a sly curiosity. The club girls are aware that they are no longer protected by invisible hands. The tide is turning against them, and all they have to rely on is the sad immortality of male desire. It might save them.

I sit here not just to escape Cairo but to escape Istanbul as well. Unlike Aksaray, this tiny enclave of bedlam is filled with Egyptian anarchy and humor. The Scarabee Alley is amateurish. On top of strange poles hang stuffed tiger toys, their tails and paws dropping earthward.

The café's plasma screens show American wrestling shows, keenly enjoyed as far as I can see by the same scarfed matrons whose disapproval does not extend to large men in bikini bottoms. I can drink Lipton with sugar and smoke for hours, and Stella is served without much discretion. When I ask about this, a neighbor tells me that Egyptians do not really regard beer as sinful alcohol. "After all," he says, "we invented it. We cannot ban what we invented."

It is probably true. Go to the Egyptian Museum, and in the room devoted to the funerary models rescued from the tomb of Meket-Re, a high official of the Middle Kingdom at Thebes, you see miniature reproductions of various workshops. Among them is a brewery, with seven little men thrusting their hands into beer fermentation jars. These perfectly preserved models of ships, workshops, and villa gardens filled with exquisitely painted fig trees are thought to embody things that the dead man valued in life and that he wanted to take with him into the afterlife. Four thousand years ago Meket-Re wanted his beer in the afterlife. In one model ship he is shown reclining in the shade of a bull hide smelling a lotus flower and listening to a minstrel.

When darkness comes, I will go to the Meame and sit at a table in a dark corner and watch a girl dance on the stage, then wander down to the tables with an insolence that is not quite lechery. The men delirious but seated, the girls there not to provide sex but to induce drinking.

Alternatively, there is a short walk to the Amira on Talaat Harb, a drinking club consisting of four rooms each with live music. It is much the same atmosphere. The music is deafening;

the men occasionally dance with the girls. The darkness almost total, and the withdrawal from the new puritanism of the country almost complete. How much one goes to bars just to escape what others laboriously refer to as *real life*. But what if that life is neither especially real nor even especially congenial? What if the society begins to close down, to narrow?

In downtown one can keep moving from *baladi* to *baladi*, because they have not yet been closed down, but you have to know where they are: using them requires a casual street knowledge that can be picked up only orally or through incessant trial and error. None of them are advertised. Most lie at the bottom of narrow unlit alleys and passageways, and no city is more a labyrinth than Cairo. Off 26th July, again, but closer to Tahrir Square, there is a strange place called the Nile Munchen, with its outdoor restaurant closed in on all sides by the backs of tenements and its ground-floor belly-dance bar. There is the touristy El-Hourreye, where the foreign journalists like to pose, and the seedier and more heartfelt Cap d'Or off Abd El-Khalik Tharwat, a den of dark varnished wood paneling and glaring light, where men pass between the all-male tables selling pistachios.

There is the splendid gloom of the Horris, a bar elevated above 26th July by a flight of steps and concealed behind anonymous glass doors, and the lofty hotel bar of the Odeon near Marouf, with its decayed oil paintings and terrible food and a terrace where sooty winds embrace the drinker.

I go one night to the Greek Club and find that it has closed. I go to the finely named Bussy Cat or to Estoril—a barman in a neat white turban—and hang about inside them like a fly that cannot decide quite where to alight; then, with a sort of desperation born of indolence, I push on to other even grimmer holes: the Alf Leila wa Leila off El Gomhoreya, the excruciating Rivera, the Victoria Hotel, or the Hawaii on Mohammed Farid. A whole evening can be spent in this misanthropic pursuit, wandering from places like Stella Bar to Carol and on to the Bar Simon or the Gemaica. But as often as not, I will come back to the calm sanity of the Cap d'Or, a bar that is not signposted and that is entered through a side door, where one can sit unmolested for hours without music or harassment, doing what one does in a bar: contemplate death and the inconsequential things that come just before it.

I love the tables here piled with nutshells, the smell of dogs and oily *ful*, and the sinister bar with its filthy bottles. The floors crunchy with the same pistachio shells. The men disheveled and worn-down looking, in their cheap leather jackets and woolly hats. There is no question that Cap d'Or is a great bar of a certain kind because there is no sexuality, no women, no flirting, no frivolity, no beauty, no cuisine on the side, no clocks, no well-dressed bohemians and pretty young men with nothing to do. It's a place of quiet but pungent pessimism, where the drinker at best can divert himself with a backgammon board but where he usually sinks sweetly into his own meditations.

As the Salafis and the Muslim Brotherhood rise to power in this traumatized republic, as the women—unimaginable two years ago—wear headscarves in the streets almost uniformly and the beards of the devout multiply, the Cairo drinker wonders how long it will be before the Scarabee Alley becomes a thing of the past. It will not happen overnight. But it is the slow, gradual changes that are the most irreversible.

That winter I was in Cairo to meet two Lebanese winemakers named Labib Kallas and André Hajj-Thomas. These two willing exiles are the bright minds behind the only winery in Egypt that grows its own grapes in the country: EgyBev.

Their company has a headquarters in the formerly affluent suburb of Heliopolis close to the airport and a winery located in the Red Sea party town of Hurghada, several hundred miles south of Cairo and roughly parallel to Luxor. Their vineyards, meanwhile, have been reclaimed from the desert land in the delta some thirty miles north of the capital, in an area that has been growing wine grapes for thousands of years—perhaps longer than anywhere on earth. In the delta once lay the vineyards of ancient Egypt. They have long disappeared, as have most of the modern vineyards established by the Greek winemaker Nestor Gianaclis a hundred years ago. Gianaclis still exists as a winery, but it is now, like most alcohol production in Egypt, owned by Heineken International. Its vineyards still operate in the same delta area as those of Labib Kallas, but Heineken imports most of its grapes for its Egyptian wines from South Africa and Lebanon. Labib, by his own reckoning, has set out to create the only range of authentic, biodynamic, and truly indigenous wines in Egypt. They are Shahrazade, Jardin du Nil, Beausoleil. His vineyards are planted with the usual international varieties, Cabernet Sauvignon, Merlot, Viognier, and Chardonnay (from which he makes the only sparkling wine in North Africa, Le Baron). But he also makes a white wine, Beausoleil, from a uniquely Egyptian grape called Bannati. It's the only Bannati wine in the world.

Labib and André are the kind of worldly, hedonistic middle-aged Lebanese who could only have been produced by a city like Beirut. They are Christians. Most of the inner staff at their company are also Christians. The workers in the vineyards, however, are Muslims, and some are even Salafi. They are not told that the grapes they are tending are meant for the production of wine. They are told they are table grapes.

As it is, many Muslim suppliers—bottlers, label makers— have told the company that their money is no longer *halal*. In the new climate of Egypt, even a label maker does not want to be associated with a winery.

We drove up on the desolate Alexandria Desert Road, which must once have been beautiful. Now it is semi-industrial, the flatlands crowded by sprawling housing developments for the affluent classes of Cairo. In recent years the city has become so unbearable, so unlivable, that those who can are building condos miles out in the desert just, as Labib puts it, "to breathe." Yet the revolution has caused this construction frenzy to pause. Around the vast vineyards that Labib and André have created over the last ten years—they are the largest single biodynamic vineyard in the world—the rows of boxlike units stand waiting for the resumption of national prosperity. It may never come.

We walked across the vineyards in cool winter sun. Vines to the horizon in every direction. The two men stopped here and there to watch the workers pruning, intervening to correct their technique. The intricate technical details of viticulture are so alien here that they have to be supervised with constant attention. The two men sometimes sleep out in the vineyards in order to do it around the clock, and over time the field hands have adapted to these peculiar demands. Yet over this whole enterprise, with its initial investment of $2 million, there hangs the inevitable uncertainty of making an alcoholic product in a country that is retreating from its secular inheritance.

André, who is now in his sixties and therefore somewhat older than Labib, lived through the Lebanese civil war of the 1970s. He has the tough weariness and joie de vivre that such experiences generate. As we strolled down a long line of Chardonnay stock, he bent down and kept picking up the sandy, slightly stony soil and filtering it through his fingers.

"I give this country another five years, and then we'll be gone. It seems quite clear to me that the Muslim Brotherhood, or even the Salafis, who are much more extreme, will come to shape the whole culture in their image. This country is 50 percent illiterate. Half the population cannot believe that a good Muslim political candidate could in any way be a bad man. They will vote for him if the imam tells them to."

Egyptians, he went on, do not think of beer as truly alcoholic. They make an exception for it and do not tax it highly. It is the national beverage, and it will probably remain so. But wine is heavily taxed, and it is not seen so favorably. Like hard liquor, it is seen as alien and European and inherently sinful. Moreover, it possesses little of the inherent allure of whisky and vodka.

The prevalence of drink in Nasser's Egypt centered on the usual beverages of the newly decolonized world. It is a colonial inheritance, as it is everywhere, and one that has until now not been repudiated. For until now almost nothing of the colonial inheritance has been repudiated except its abstract ideas about race. For all the rhetoric that liberation created, the whisky and soda remain alongside the electricity grids, the roads, and the airports. Only Islam has begun to roll back that tide, and it, too, will keep most of the goodies but not the booze, the music, or the film.

The Egyptian Revolution, meanwhile, has not made Labib and André optimistic. There is no institutional core to the society and none can be created out of nothing, and certainly not overnight. It is a vacuum, it has been a vacuum for half a century. Into the original vacuum of the Revolution of 1952 the army moved, as always happens. They have run the country ever since. Egypt has decayed decade by decade. Forty million illiterates, and a city that is fragmenting, falling into pieces. Into dust and ruin.

I asked them out of curiosity whether Cairo could be rebuilt as Beirut has been, by the construction company Solidere, after the Lebanese civil war. They shrugged. The civil war in Lebanon destroyed Beirut. The historic city all but vanished. To rebuild it as Solidere has done, with shining skyscrapers created by the company's total territorial control of the city center, was possible there. Cairo is the opposite. It is decaying, but it has not been destroyed. Its decay will therefore go on forever. It is entropy, not reinvention. Egyptians, if you want to look on the bright side, are not the kind to slaughter one another over differences.

"But in the meantime," Labib concluded, as we walked around piles of his homemade biodynamic compost, "we are the only genuine wine left in Egypt. Yet we could not get a permit from the local Giza authorities to put our winery next to our vineyards. It has to be four hundred miles away!"

Nevertheless, it's only a one-hour flight to Hurghada. The next day we were there, driving from the beach town to the far more exclusive resort development of El Gouna, half an hour north on the coast. It is there that the Lebanese wine men both live and work—the winery is next door to the Arabian-themed adobe faux-village built around a marina. They have bought condos in the Arabian complexes, between which cobbled alleys attempt to evoke the narrow streets of a meticulously restored medina in the Gulf.

The style here is very Dubai. Shops, restaurants, clubs, nautical equipment stores, antique outlets all merge into an ethnic mall executed in apparently local materials and quietly furnished with Wi-Fi. El Gouna is a gated community where everything has been built from scratch. For the Cairene rich, it is a desirable fantasy, an escape into efficiency and dustlessness. Here the gilded young come on their EgyptAir charters, dressed in Dutti and Burberry and chattering in the new language of Arabenglish. The marina is filled with luxury yachts registered in ports all over the world. Alcohol flows freely in every outlet.

El Gouna is one of those representations of the West, one of its outposts in a far-flung corner of an Islamic desert landscape, that continue to nourish an idea of a secular civilization that is otherwise perceived as dying by the very people who are seduced by it. The culture of the drinkers, of the free people who can do as they please, is the same culture whose maternity wards are empty, whose public finances are in a death spiral, and whose self-absorbed banalities no longer enchant those who were once their most avid admirers.

We visited the winery during the day. It is a state-of-the-art place, similar in every way to comparable wineries in the West. Here we sat among the steel fermentation tanks and drank through vertical tastings of their offerings, including the low-end Moon Reef, sold as an "all inclusive" wine in Egypt's Club Med resorts, and the Le Baron rosé *méthode champenoise*.

Labib described taking his wines to an international trade fair in Montpellier. Medals, praise, bafflement were the result: an Egyptian wine is not an easy sell. Egyptians themselves are glumly skeptical. They refer to their homegrown wines as Château Panadol. The very idea is tenuous, fragile. Labib even makes a pretty good grappa, but Egyptians will not drink it. Their arak is their best bet.

But even arak is not the national drink of Egypt. Beer is. At night, however, seated in the marina restaurants with their resolute American food, we drank the Jardin du Nil reds and the elegant white Bannati Beausoleil, and the two men mused that an eventual return to Lebanon was all but inevitable. But what about a displacement to the West? I asked.

No, that was now suddenly a little less appealing than it had once been. The West was saturated, aging, overtaxed. It was not particularly enjoyable as a place. And they were Arabs. They wanted to be among the Arabs. They wanted to change the Arabs by refining their palates. Besides, making wine in Egypt was at least a novelty, it was an adventure. It was even possible that one day in the future, the Egyptian middle class would tire of endless strawberry juices and convert to wines made in their own delta. It depended on whether prosperity ever returned to the land.

"Did you see," André said one night, "that member of the Egyptian parliament who began singing prayers in the middle of a parliamentary session? It's gone viral on YouTube in Egypt. It's almost a brawl. He won't shut up, and the speaker has to shout him down. It was Mamdouh Ismail, a Salafist politician. This is the way it is going. They can't even discuss normal things in the parliament without these lunatics bursting into prayer and disrupting everything. They would happily tear up all the vineyards we have planted, and they have said that they will."

On the marina of El Gouna stands a renowned nightclub called Loca Loca. Its booming music can be heard all over the village, and through its windows we could see bodies writhing to rave music.

"There seems," Labib said, "to be something in the Egyptian character that might prevent that happening. I might be wrong. They used to say the same thing about Iran."

"But Iran's history is not over," I said. "Like Egypt, it is much older than Islam. Like Lebanon, for that matter."

"It's only Arabia that is not older than Islam, and even that

is actually. But here the awareness of ancient Egypt is so over-
whelming. It will always be there."

The beautiful little painted figures of beer makers of the
Old Kingdom, with their supple breasts and hips: the brewers
of Meket-Re are not the only ones in the Egyptian Museum
in Cairo.

"Here," he went on, "the drinking of something like beer
was thousands of years old before Islam arrived. It had gone too
deep. I don't know if they drank beer in medieval Cairo, but I'd
bet they did."

"I think," André put in, "that they drink beer in this country
exactly as the ancients did. As a kind of surrogate water. It's not
ghettoized as alcohol."

"It's still the national drug."

Regardless of the alcoholic habits of, say, the Fatimid period,
I thought then of Kerényi and his claim for a possible Egyptian
origin of beer and mead. The fermentations at the time of the
reappearance of the Dog Star in July. The magical atmosphere
of intoxication. If it had been drunk here for five thousand years,
or even more, it could not be proscribed. It was strange, too, to
think that mead was a staple drink of the English almost until
modern times, but that today it is virtually the only alcoholic
drink that cannot be obtained as a commercial product. *Meodu*,
the Anglo-Saxons called it. The fermented timeless honey drink
of the Nile.

Later, we went to Loca Loca and drank toxicly strong cocktails. The drinks were so powerful that the crowd seemed more
stoned on mescal than drunk on alcohol. It was a sexual crowd, a

pickup crowd, mostly Egyptian, Lebanese, and European, and it drank in a hard, purposeful, self-forgetting way. The symbiosis of bodily, erotic freedom and alcohol once again flared up. Or as the Earl of Rochester had it:

Cupid, and Bacchus, my Saints are,
May drink, and Love, still reign,
With Wine, I wash away my cares,
And then to Cunt again.

Back in Cairo, I spent some days alone at the Windsor, venturing nightly down to the decaying bar and its trophied antlers and drinking cold glasses of disgusting Omar Khayyam with plates of hummus. The place was often empty. Marco leaned his elbows on the bar, and we talked about the old days. Ah, how magnificent Cairo was then. A lake of precious distillations at which intellectuals and men of taste could sip at their leisure like glorious honeybees. It was all over now.

Where were the intellectuals and the men of taste? Where was the grace and the finesse of yore? The deep sophistication of Egypt must still be there somewhere, like a hidden river waiting to reemerge into daylight. It could never totally run dry, since from the time of the pharaoh Djoser on, it had never done so. But there were periods of darkness. Periods of dry.

On the pavements of 26th July, I sometimes passed old-time liquor stores, tiny dens that reminded me of the permit rooms of Pakistan. There was a larger one called Orphanides, obviously once Greek-owned; a few blocks away stood a corner store called Humbaris, whose window was filled with unusual indigenous brews that I had not seen before, not even in the *baladis*. Here there were bottles of Zabiba Extra arak, as well as Rucard and Zahia, the latter with a lovely label of palms on a sand-yellow background. There were Grant's and Highland whisky, Biulli's—described as "Old Egyptian Whiskey"—and Wadie Horse (a deliberate play, I assume, on White Horse), and yet another "Egyptian" Scotch called Chivas Regal. There was a thing called Red Greec Soldier (sic), which might have been an ouzo, and Marcel J & B whisky, described on its label as "A Blwnd of the Super Old Drink Egyption" (sic). There was a potion called the Red Barrel Brand, identified as a French type "Matignonne," and dust-covered bottles of a thing known as Valentine's "Marceil." Even more unnerving was an evil-looking squat bottle with a blue label marked "Vodka of Cairo." Five Egyptian pounds *la bouteille,* it said. Instant death in a lonely hotel room.

But among these native oddities, which evade by their very nature the 450 percent tax that is levied on alcoholic imports, I found at Orphanides a bottle of Le Baron rosé "champagne." I went into the store to buy it.

Inside, the radio blasted Islamic music and prayers, and the staff, astonished to see me, craned forward as they tried to decipher my appalling Arabic. Yes, they had the champagne, but they would have to dig it out of the storeroom. I waited, and they brought me a cup of tea. Perhaps they hoped I would buy a second bottle and maybe a bit of Cairo vodka thrown in. Eventually, however, the Le Baron appeared, heavily dusted like most of the bottles there, and it was wiped down with a cloth and handed to me rolled in newspaper. I took it home through downtown to the Windsor, went up to my chilled room with Mustafa in the elevator, and put the bottle in my ancient fridge. An hour later it was cold.

I turned on the ancient heaters and opened the windows. Then I went to the sinister black phone sitting on the bedside table. The Windsor phones have no numbers or dials, and they seem to have been inside these rooms since about 1950. You pick up the receiver, there is a soft crackling, and eventually a voice says "Salaam." I asked for an ice bucket. I asked for it as a joke, in fact, but the reply was "Right away, sir." One of the ancient staff members in a djellaba and turban delivered it with thunderous punctuality. I placed the bucket next to the bed and opened the Le Baron as the evening prayers started up. There is something life-affirming about peeling back the foil cap of a champagne bottle and prying open the wires. I remembered that someone once praised a book of Henry Miller by saying that reading it was like listening to all the champagne corks in the world going off at the same time. A book, in other words, that made you glad that you were alive. The Le Baron was fresh and acidic and well made. It may have been the only North African sparkling wine, but it was a pretty good one, a noble effort to do something tricky and difficult. I had the feeling that Labib made it for his own pleasure more than anything. It had his warmth at its core, his fear for the future.

Ten minutes past six. I drank it slowly in bed, and soon the night air came up off the street, with its taste of hundred-year-old trees and *shish* smoke and—for some reason—buttered popcorn. I made a silent toast to my mother, who would have enjoyed drinking it with me in that fusty, darkened room where the shutters were falling off their hinges. One never ends where one began, and over those two years of drinking in countries that by long tradition had decided against the corrosive pleasures of alcohol, I had come to love my 6:10 drink more than anything in the inanimate world. I enjoyed it more here than I did elsewhere precisely because here its enigma was more fragile, more lucidly despised and feared. The reasons for hating it are all valid. But by the same token they are not really reasons at all. For in the end alcohol is merely us, a materialization of our own nature. To repress it is to repress something that we know about ourselves but cannot celebrate or even accept. It is like having a dance partner we cannot trust with our wallet.

The room filled with carbide light from the street. More than at any moment in those two years, I felt the words of Pindar coming back as I drank through that entire bottle of Egyptian sparkling. The words described the god Dionysus: *hagnon phengos oporas,* "the pure light of high summer." It was a phrase I could not forget, and I suppose it denoted something that I had been looking for all along. That light seemed to fill me right then, pouring out of those delicate rose-colored bubbles swimming at the edge of a cheap wineglass soiled by a dead ant. The word *alcohol* now seemed distant and irrelevant to this mood.

And so I thought back, as I stepped gingerly into that gentle drunken state, to the time I had lain in a field of English wheat and waited for a combine harvester to chop me into pieces. I must have known something then that my body, at least, chose not to forget thereafter. It was a sort of forgiveness.

By the time I emptied the bottle, I was half asleep, and when I woke, the Windsor staff had cleared away the ice bucket and the glass and the bottle itself. My mother had left as well, and I was alone in the sunlight waiting for a clock somewhere to strike six yet again, as it would every day until the final call of all.

New from
Lawrence Osborne

"A searing portrait of addiction and despair."

—*Publishers Weekly*

AVAILABLE WHEREVER BOOKS ARE SOLD